TRAC
THE HISTORY OF
HOUSES

— TREVOR YORKE —

COUNTRYSIDE BOOKS
NEWBURY BERKSHIRE

First published 2011
© Trevor Yorke 2011

COUNTRYSIDE BOOKS
3 Catherine Road
Newbury, Berkshire

To view our complete range of books,
please visit us at
www.countrysidebooks.co.uk

ISBN 978 1 84674 265 1

Photographs and illustrations by the author

Designed by Peter Davies, Nautilus Design
Produced through MRM Associates Ltd., Reading
Typeset by CJWT Solutions, St Helens
Printed by Information Press, Oxford

CONTENTS

SECTION II

SECTION III

Introduction

We are a nation passionate about old houses. We stand in awe of the grandest, renovate the modest and admire the quaintest. From rural cottages to urban terraces, our deep-rooted love affair with rusticated façades, traditional materials, and structures which are contorted by age, constantly draws our attention to period properties. The bond is greater than just a pleasing visual effect; every house has a story to tell reflecting the personal ambitions of its past owners and the history of its town or village. When we own or look around a house, questions come to mind such as 'Who built it?', 'How old is it?', 'Why does it look like this?' Our vast heritage of building styles, regional materials and structural forms can be bewildering; a situation not helped by publications on architecture tending to become preoccupied with technical details and confusing terms. This book, however, is intended to introduce the beginner to the subject and enhance the knowledge of those with some understanding of it. I have used my own drawings and photographs to explain how houses have developed and the methods by which you can find out more about their history.

I first became interested in the subject when I bought a property that simply looked odd! I knew a bit about architecture from years of illustrating buildings and it seemed to me that the roof was too shallow, the timbers too broad and the windows were all wrong for the size of the house. As it turned out my suspicions were right, it was half of a much larger 16th-century farmhouse, the other part of which had been demolished in the 19th century, and a row of workers' cottages built in its place. This began an obsession for me with trying to date and understand houses from their exterior structure, decorative details and interior form and then attempting to confirm my interpretation through documentary sources. You can't beat the thrill of finding an important detail, uncovering something in a dusty loft or discovering a vital piece of information which suddenly puts a piece into place, and it can be just as rewarding to research a small Victorian terrace as it can an imposing Georgian manor house.

The book starts with a short preface which suggests a method to use when tracing the history of a house before looking in detail at its relationship with the town or village, the changing structure and styles through the centuries, how to date a house from the materials and decorative details, and how to recognise the period features inside. The first section of the book uses photographs, drawings and diagrams to show you how you can identify the period in which a house was built and the features which can tell you more about how it developed. The second section outlines the most useful sources for researching houses, beginning with a basic listing of those which can easily be accessed locally or online. The next chapter looks at archives further afield which can help in a more advanced search of the property, while the final part lists sources which are more useful for finding out who lived there. The Quick Reference Guide at the end has a list of websites and books which can help take your research further; a time chart which puts periods, styles and details in an easy-to-understand format; and a glossary of the more unfamiliar terms.

It does not matter if you just want to know more about the buildings around you or whether you want to find out the complete history of your own house. The book makes no assumptions about age or size: anything from a Tudor timber-framed cottage to a 1930s' semi is included. It is intended to empower the reader to identify some of the principal features of period houses and to be familiar with the sources of research, but above all to enjoy the pleasure which comes from discovering something new about a property which can open up its past secrets.

Trevor Yorke

Drawings of a timber-framed, Regency and an Arts and Crafts house – with labels of the main features which you will come across when looking into the history of houses.

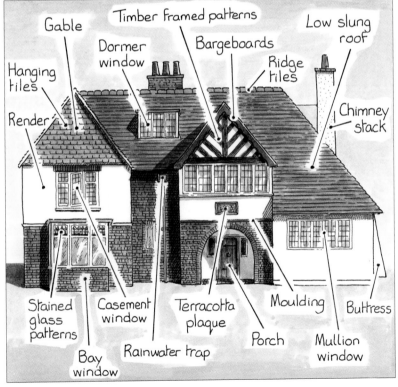

PREFACE
Tracing the History of a House

The English house comes in all manner of shapes and sizes. From Georgian terraces towering four or five storeys over urban pavements to humble thatched cottages rambling down village lanes. There are stout, square farmhouses standing proudly in the centre of their fields and tiny two-up, two-downs squeezed within monotonous rows of Victorian streets. Some display the latest styles while others imitate the past. Some 1930s' estates will have flat-roofed, white-rendered, modern houses for the more adventurous resident, next to ones with mock timber-framing, bay windows and herringbone brickwork, creating a more reassuring, traditional façade.

This variety of form is further enhanced by the great diversity of building materials found within our relatively small island. Grey granites in Cornwall, rusty limestones in the Cotswolds, and gritty sandstones in the Pennines contrast with black and white timber-framing in Cheshire, white weatherboarding in Kent and colourful mud walls in Devon. Even when these traditional, local materials (referred to as vernacular) were superseded by brick during the 19th century, the qualities of the clay used for the bricks still coloured the finished product, from the yellows in London to the rich reds in Manchester. The properties of the different stones, bricks and timber also help shape the building, in some cases determining the form of the structure, thickness of the walls and size of openings within them, while the pitch of the roof (how steep or shallow it is) relates to the wide variety of coverings which have been used in the past.

Further confusion is created by many houses being deceptive; some copying past styles with a cladding of rustic features disguising its modern structure, while others were designed to make the building appear to be of better quality than it was. Regency brick terraces were clad with a render known as stucco which, when scoured and coloured, appeared like fashionable Bath or Portland stone, despite the walls beneath being of a much cheaper material and dubious construction – this is the time when the phrase *jerry building* was first coined (from a nautical term for temporary rigging). In the late Victorian period the revival by the Arts and Crafts movement, where traditional methods and materials were used, inspired speculative builders (those who speculated by building first and then selling or renting the

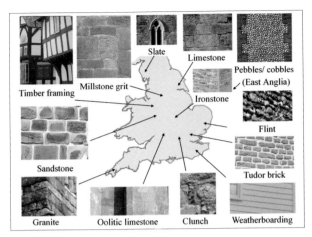

FIG 0.1: *A map of England showing the distinctive regional building materials which are characteristic of certain areas.*

property afterwards) to cover their standard terraces and semis with all manner of traditional finishes to imitate them.

This wide selection of forms, materials and our habit of jumbling it up by reviving past styles can make it difficult to identify the date when a house was built. However, underneath this apparent confusion there are plans and structural types which were common in a certain period, regulations which changed the appearance of buildings for a known length of time and styles and decorative details which can be pinpointed to a particular date. We are also fortunate enough in this country that the lack of warfare and revolution on our soil has resulted in the preservation of government, ecclesiastic, manorial and estate documentation which can be invaluable for research. Some of the documentation can help turn an approximate dating from the visual evidence into a definite one and uncover names of past residents and owners (before the First World War most houses were rented out by the owner who may never have lived in the building itself).

Whether the house you are interested in is ancient or modern, grand or humble, urban or rural, it will still have a history to unfold. Do not think because it is a small, plain property or it was built in the last hundred years that it is not worth investigating. There is as much fascinating evidence to be uncovered from a post-war prefab about life in 1940s' Britain as can be discovered about a timber-framed house from the Tudor Age. This book treats all periods and types of houses with equal respect and will enlighten the reader in the important aspects which help date most houses which can be seen today.

BEFORE YOU START

The following chapters are laid out in a sequence which makes a logical introduction to tracing the history of a house, starting with visual evidence in the first section and then documentation in the second. Before starting research on a property, however, it is important to consider a few suggestions on the methods used and your initial approach to the task:

1. Work from the whole to the part. Firstly, try to find out about the town or village in which the house is set, and then work down to more specific information about the street and the buildings themselves. It is all too easy to assume the building is of a certain date because of a decorative detail or to focus upon a known previous owner without first stepping back and looking at the overall picture.

2. Keep a record of everything you find. Don't discard any facts, names or details you collect. Even if you only do a basic search at this stage, you might find the facts useful if you go back to the project later. Stand back every so often and put any new information into place. Perhaps make a chart of occupants like a family tree or list information found by date. It's amazing how many times this sort of organising suddenly links pieces of the puzzle together or highlights something worthy of more research.

3. Do not set yourself a timescale. You might discover all you want within a few weeks of research but if you get hooked or the mystery deepens, months can turn into years, a time well worth the wait, especially if you have that eureka moment when you find a dusty old document that puts the last piece of the jigsaw into place.

4. Find out first what research has already been carried out on the property. Ask neighbours and previous owners if they know anything regarding the history of the house. Local history groups or libraries may also be aware of work carried out while solicitors or estate agents who have handled the sale of the property, will often have some knowledge of its past. Should you find work has been carried out then do not let it put you off your own research, you may be able to go further back in time or discover more; although the previous research can help save time by highlighting useful sources and revealing previous names of the house or occupants. When approaching some of the above people, always be polite and remember your requests will not be their top priority. Emails and letters (with a stamped addressed envelope) may be the best first approach.

5. Draw up a plan of the house with measurements. It does not have to be to scale, although this helps, but it is important to record the overall dimensions of the building, the size of rooms and details such as the thickness of walls. It can also be beneficial to know dimensions of the plot and the acreage if it is rural. This plan will be useful to help you evaluate the evidence you find when searching through documents, as the house may only be identifiable by size and position rather than name.

FIG 0.2: *It can be important to measure the house and record it on a plan since the area of the property, width of frontage and size of rooms may help to identify your house in old documents where its name is often not mentioned.*

6. Make a photographic record of the house. It is crucial at this early stage to look at the house in detail inside and out, taking time to notice any signs of blocked up openings, changes in stone, brickwork, timber and any decorative details, odd gaps or features. Take photographs of all elevations (especially sides and the rear where the least change is likely to have happened), the inside of rooms and any of the details which may be of interest. It is also important to explore and record what you find inside the loft as this can often help date a building and identify whether the property has been altered or extended. Keep copies of these photographs as they will be useful when comparing with other properties, showing them to an expert in the field and researching away from home.

By using the photographs and plan of the house, the next task should be to try to date the building from the physical evidence you have recorded. The following chapters give an outline of how the structure, style and interior details may have changed through time. This will help you to recognise the sequence of construction (even houses only a hundred years old may have been extended and altered a number of times) and thus arrive at an approximate period in which the original structure was built.

FIG 0.3: *Above are photos of some of the features which are worth noting when studying your own house. Look for changes in brickwork (left), blocked doors (centre) and altered roof lines (right).*

SECTION I

HISTORY
AND
DEVELOPMENT

CHAPTER 1
A Brief History of Housing

To understand how the property in which you are interested may have originally appeared and the status of its early occupants, it is first important to understand how housing has developed.

Medieval and Tudor Housing

In most parts of the country, ordinary houses built before the 17th century were comprised of only one room in which to eat and sleep and, depending on access to good building practices and materials, may have stood for only a generation or two. What we regard today as a quaint cottage would have been a large, desirable property in medieval and Tudor times, its two storeys standing proudly over the humble hovels around it.

Most houses in this period would have been built by commissioning a carpenter or builder to erect the property to rough specifications (if the skills to do so did not exist within the family). The original layout and size of the house would have reflected the desires, demands and status of its first occupants, while its structure would have been vernacular, formed from materials sourced locally and methods

FIG 1.1: *Most urban terraces from the mid-17th century were erected by speculative builders, small-scale companies constructing only a short row of houses at a time (note these terraces built in pairs). With the direct contact between builder and occupant now being lost, the standard could drop and corners were cut as the tenant was unlikely to see it being built. This problem was made worse in earlier examples since the lease for the land was very short and so there was little incentive for houses to be built to last.*

passed down from older generations. It was only from the late 17th century onwards that it became common for builders to speculate, usually erecting a small number of houses in the latest style to pass onto a landlord, or find tenants themselves, before moving on to the next project.

A notable change in the quality and size of houses occurred as the population started to grow and incomes increased during the Tudor period. Beginning in the south-east in the late 16th century and spreading slowly across the country until the late 18th century, this 'Great Rebuilding' as it is now termed, resulted in better quality, permanent housing for an increasing number of farmers, merchants and skilled workers. It can be important to know your local history if you think the house you are researching is of this antiquity as it is likely that it will date to the rebuilding in your area which varied depending upon industry, trade and agricultural improvement. For instance, parts of Suffolk and the Cotswolds, which became prosperous with the wool trade, had new two-storey houses built as early as the late 1400s while the Pennine district of Lancashire only started the process in the late 1700s as the cotton industry expanded.

Rebuilding can also be dated to the aftermath of a major fire, a blight which affected many towns and cities in the past, devastating the largely timber-built housing. The most famous was the Great Fire of London of 1666 which is

FIG 1.2: *When a medieval town was first laid out or an area redeveloped or extended, the properties facing the road or market area were divided up into distinctive long, thin burgage plots. These were laid out using an English rod, perch or pole, approximately 16½ ft long, and many urban plots today can still be found to be 1 or 1½ rod lengths, or divisible by this dimension (another common dimension was one-eighth of a mile, approximately 220 yards, which was the length of a ploughed strip in a field, the furrow-long, or as we know it 'the furlong'). These regular planned layouts (surprisingly common in villages as well as most old towns) were gradually broken down from the 15th century. Firstly the Black Death had devastated the population so those who survived took over neighbouring property and then as growth began in the Tudor period, spaces like the market, dissolved monastic property, urban fields and orchards and castle grounds were built on before later the town expanded out of its medieval boundary. The plan of Leek in Staffordshire above highlights in yellow the probable area originally laid out by the local abbey in the medieval period, with its distinctive long thin burgage strips (bottom right), while the later additions filling in the original much larger market space are shown in orange.*

FIG 1.3: NANTWICH, CHESHIRE.
Most of the fine black and white timber-framed buildings here can be dated to the immediate years after 1581 when a major fire devastated the town.

important not only for the vast scale of the destruction but also for the actions taken afterwards to ensure that it did not happen again. The king and his authorities had long tried to control housing quality within built-up areas to reduce the risk of fire but with little success. Now, in the wake of this event, a building act was introduced which not only reinforced bans on using timber and thatch and laid down the sizes of houses and streets, but also employed inspectors to make sure they were enforced. The forms of urban housing over the following centuries were shaped by this and by subsequent acts which sought to further reduce the risk of fire spreading. Until the late 18th century, however, they only applied to London, and were usually adopted by local authorities as good practice sometime afterwards, so do be cautious when using these changes to help date a house.

Up until the early 1600s, most large houses were designed and built by a master mason or carpenter. It was only as the 17th century progressed that an architect, usually an amateur gentleman rather than a trained professional, became responsible solely for the design. By the late 18th century this had become a trade, with professionals creating and publishing new styles and plans, with builders of smaller houses further down the ladder trying to

---

Building Acts:

1667 *Building act categorized houses based on their total interior area and tied it into set widths of the streets, imposed restrictions on certain flammable materials and appointed building inspectors to visit the site so this regulation was largely adhered to.*

1707 *Building act banned wooden cornices from the façade and brick parapets were extended to 2½ feet above floor level of attic/loft.*

1709 *Building act recessed sash boxes 4 inches back (both the 1707 and 1709 acts had generally taken effect elsewhere in the country by the 1730s).*

1774 *Building act (again at first for London) not only specified new rates for houses but also set sash boxes behind brickwork, specified the quality of materials, the thickness of walls and most aspects of construction.*

emulate them. Not only did they have to contend with the ever-increasing number of regulations, but also taxes imposed upon the property: window tax from the 1690s (calculated on the number of windows the house had) and brick tax in the wake of the American War of Independence (worked out on the quantity used in construction). These taxes encouraged builders to cut corners in order to use fewer bricks and to create blank, recessed openings to maintain symmetry but without having to pay for a window. The repeal of these taxes in the 1850s led in part to an explosion in decorative brickwork and bay windows.

Rural Housing

The majority of people in the 17th and 18th centuries still lived in the country and worked on the land. The villages they lived in tended to develop into two key types which were reflected in the housing of the period. Some were open, where there was little restriction on building and a lack of interest from a local lord so houses could appear gathered around industrial workings, on wasteland and commons, with little attention paid to facilities and appearance. Others were closed, with the lord of the manor maintaining a tight control over all aspects of village life, encouraging undesirables to leave but building better quality homes for those whom he decided could stay. Many villages of the former type still retain their rather haphazard development, often based around an industry, quarrying or mining, with cottages of different qualities and, often today, having been much extended. Many of our most attractive villages, however, owe their appearance to the restrictions imposed by a strong-minded lord, and in these closed settlements the houses, sometimes with a unified architectural theme, are more likely to be in their original form.

FIG 1.4: *In some medieval villages you were allowed to build a house on common land if it was sufficiently complete that a fire was burning in the grate by evening on the day you started. This resulted in so much encroachment that a law was passed in 1589 to try and restrict it but in many areas it continued as it suited farmers to have labourers close at hand. Some houses today may have replaced earlier longhouses like this example which were established this way.*

Much of this new rural housing was built due to dramatic changes in many villages during this period. The open-field system, which had dominated medieval settlements from Dorset in the south, up through the Midlands and into Yorkshire, had been gradually eroded ever since the 15th century, with many villages having their lands enclosed with agreement reached on the new distribution of land within the community. However, with the drive for agricultural improvement in the

FIG 1.5: *The home of the local priest had formerly been a humble building often within the churchyard, but from the 17th century as the career began to be seen as one suitable for the second son of the nobility, this new generation of clergy expected a finer house to reflect their status. Large vicarages often date from the late 17th and 18th centuries, with symmetrical façades and two or three storeys. The revival of the Church of England in the 1830s and 40s resulted in the creation of new parishes better suited to serve the needs of a rapidly shifting population and new asymmetrical vicarages usually in a more appropriate Gothic style appeared in towns and villages, as in this example.*

18th century, a new wave of enclosures, this time ratified by parliamentary act, resulted in new farmhouses being built or existing ones extended out into the fields, while their old farms back in the village were often divided up to form workers' cottages (look for a large central chimney stack with later smaller ones either side). Another dramatic action was when the lord of the manor decided he needed a new country house and park set a comfortable distance from the village. Quite often it was the village which had to shift! The offending settlement was usually removed and a new one built a short distance away, with fine-quality housing forming an attractive entrance for visitors to the manor (some were designed by the same architect who created the main house). Many rural houses were built or had changes made to them due to these actions in this period, and finding out more about local enclosures and emparkments can reveal their history.

Improvements in transport could also have a marked effect on rural housing. The creation of turnpike trusts in the 18th century resulted in many new and existing routes becoming busy roads. New inns and hotels were built or altered to appear more modern in order to attract passing trade, with many of the houses now lining these old routes being dated to these prosperous times. River navigations, canals and then railways also tended to result in new housing being built, sometimes a row of terraces close to the route for workers, other times owing to the village expanding towards the wharf or station through the increase in trade. Knowing when these forms of transport arrived in the settlement can be fundamental to dating and understanding many rural and urban properties.

FIG 1.6: EDENSOR, DERBY. *This model village was created on a new site between 1838–1842 by the Duke of Devonshire who wished it out of sight of Chatsworth House. The houses were planned in part by his gardener Joseph Paxton (later designer of the Crystal Palace) and were in a style which featured in J.C.Loudon's* Encyclopaedia of Cottage, Farm and Villa Architecture *which was very influential in house design in the early to mid-19th century.*

Victorian Housing

A more efficient agricultural system was one of the reasons for a notable rise in population (or at least a drop in the death rate especially among the young) in the second half of the 18th century, which was a key factor in powering the Industrial Revolution. The loss of land and forced eviction, due to enclosure and emparkment, turned many smallholders into casual labourers. Vast numbers of them began making the move from country to town where they could get better pay and often better living conditions (a mill worker in Lancashire could earn twice as much as a farm labourer in parts of the south). During the 19th century this drift into urban areas continued, with families usually having to share a single room within an old house, or perhaps a family would have its own back-to-back which, although initially would have been welcomed, soon turned into a slum. However, by the end of the Victorian period, the wealth of the country had

FIG 1.7: *Old toll houses with distinctive angled bay fronts so the occupant could clearly see traffic coming in both directions are a characteristic feature of turnpike roads. These single or two storey buildings, usually with low hipped roofs can be dated from records of the trusts and their transfer into private hands which often took place when they were dissolved.*

generally filtered down to the working classes and those in a good job could expect to rent a small two-up, two-down terraced house.

As towns and cities expanded due to trade and industry, the demand for new housing grew and was only met by the mass production of building and the lower transport costs offered by the canals, and then the railways. In this Victorian period, vernacular buildings were replaced by houses built to standardised plans made popular through books and magazines. They used bricks and slate from all over the country and the fashionable decoration for the façades was ordered from a catalogue. But most houses were still designed and built by local craftsmen. Architects for the finer houses were usually based in the town while the builders were often small-scale companies that erected short rows of houses within a longer terrace (upon close inspection, you may see breaks in the brickwork or narrow gaps where one builder stopped and another (or the same) continued at a later date). Although, in principle, dating houses from this period is made easier by distinctive styles which were changing quickly, the range of ideas could still take some time to spread from London to distant areas. Also there were some builders who continued to stick with the old designs, while others imitated the latest style before it had become commonplace in the capital.

This Victorian urban expansion around a Georgian and earlier core was usually done with little control on the overall planning. A landowner would sell off pockets of his land, or he would invite a builder to develop his plot with a simple grid of streets laid out within its bounds. The outer edge of the original area can sometimes still be traced on maps, with the name of the landowner recorded in a street name. Housing began to stretch out further onto farmland, which was cheaper than land in existing urban areas, especially in regions suffering agricultural depression in the

FIG 1.8: *During the late 19th century, despite Leek being a rather remote mill town off the beaten track, it was an important centre for fabric production and dyeing such that William Morris spent time here perfecting natural colours. Thomas Wardle whose dye works Morris was working at had this house built in a style which would become common in London and elsewhere in the 1880s and 1890s, yet this design by the leading architect Richard Norman Shaw was built in 1873. This illustrates the haphazard way ideas spread and how it can be important to understand the history of your area to identify boom periods or links with national movements or important individuals.*

FIG 1.9: *A simplified map showing how towns can expand out from their medieval centre, swallowing up old farms, hamlets and villages along the way (see Fig 1.12). Generally the bulk of older properties will be nearer the centre and the most recent furthest out. Areas also changed in status within the town. The centre was fashionable in Georgian times but during the 19th century the wealthy sought more privacy and moved out to suburbs, leaving their old homes to be split up into cheaper housing and flats only for them to be restored to former glory in the past 40 years.*

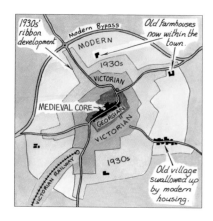

late 19th century. These new suburban estates were only practical because railway, underground and tram lines linked them to the old centres (many houses were built in anticipation of a new station being built, or sites were developed by the railway company itself). It was from this period that housing estates were designed with consideration being given to their overall appearance, with open space provided and greenery planted. In the first decades of the 20th century, this innovation blossomed into the Garden City movement which, in turn, inspired 1930s' suburban developments and early town planning.

Housing for the working classes gradually began to improve in the later Victorian period, although areas of poor and insanitary housing and back-to-backs were still a problem well into the 1960s. Regulators turned their attention from fire prevention to health and sanitation, and most building acts at the time dealt with improvements to water supply, drainage and sewerage. With little help from the authorities most early attempts at clearing the slums came from benevolent individuals, factory owners and charities. Tenement flats, financed by philanthropist George Peabody, were an early attempt at accommodating the poor. Housing developments like those at Port Sunlight on Merseyside and Bournville in Birmingham took it a stage further, providing spacious surroundings and green spaces for houses with the luxury of their own toilet. It was not until after the First World War that pressure, especially from the multitude of returning soldiers, forced the authorities to finance council estates, with the intention of clearing the worst slum areas.

Twentieth-Century Housing

The inter-war years were a period of great contrasts. Many old industries struggled to compete on the world market, and the towns and cities which they dominated saw declining quality of life and little new housing. However, where the new light

FIG 1.10: BEDFORD PARK, WEST LONDON. *This was the first notable large-scale development aimed specifically at the middle class artisan and built in the late 1870s and 1880s close to the new station at Turnham Green. It was set amongst tree-lined streets with existing roads and features retained; an important consideration to the Arts and Crafts movement which was emerging at the time. The white-painted woodwork, Dutch gables and fine red-brick are distinctive of the Queen Anne style and are frequently found on middle class terraces in the 1880s and 1890s.*

industries such as car manufacture, chemicals and electrical goods were established (mainly in the Midlands and the South-East), huge new suburban estates followed. Larger semi-detached houses provided greater privacy and the middle classes were now demanding space to grow vegetables and flowers and, for the first time, they were taking on mortgages to buy their new properties rather than just renting them. Those fortunate enough to live on a council estate could marvel at the spaciousness

FIG 1.11: *The plan of a road or estate can also be a clue to its date. Squares were fashionable in the Georgian and Regency period, straight grids of roads in the Victorian era, while inter war houses were laid out along distinctive curving and radiating tree-lined streets. The names can also be a clue. Street, Terrace and Villas were popular during the 19th century, while Crescents, Cul-de-sacs and Avenues were common in the inter war years. This plan illustrates the contrast in layout and names between Victorian housing (bottom) and 1920s housing (top).*

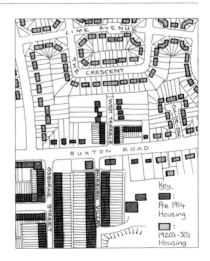

and conveniences they now had, although the higher rents, the distance from their family, and the strict rules enforced by the dreaded inspectors encouraged some to 'jump ship' and go back to city-centre slums. This suburban expansion was rapid and largely unregulated. Houses meandered along main roads far into the country, linking villages to towns – a ribbon development which lost many rural communities their identities.

After the Second World War, the authorities faced a severe problem. Not only did they have to accommodate all those who had lost their homes to bombing; cope with a baby-boom with more young couples needing a home; continue with the clearances of slums; and also respond to the expectations people now had for better housing; but also they had to achieve it with the country bankrupt! Prefabricated bungalows and concrete semi-detached houses were a short-term solution, along with the creation of flats and bedsits in old Victorian and Georgian terraces. It was not until the 1950s and '60s, however, that new housing was built on a scale which could alleviate the problem. This was only possible on a tight budget by using new methods, materials and adopting a modern style of architecture: plain, simple structures with panels of hanging tiles or wooden planks to make it appear more traditional (a common theme throughout the history of English housing). The open-plan interior which was advertised as new in these houses was, in effect, reintroducing the medieval open hall. In a way, housing had come full circle!

FIG 1.12: *The orientation or alignment of a house can also be a clue to whether it is older than neighbouring properties. As towns expanded in the 19th and 20th centuries they often spread over existing rural properties and farms (see Fig 1.9) and it is common to see an odd building stepped back or on a slightly different alignment to neighbouring houses indicating that it may be older (as in this example). In the past when it was believed that the southerly wind brought pestilence, the house could be laid out with a windowless gable end facing that direction. Also when going down a hill it was easier to excavate the shorter side dimension so houses have a gable end onto the road in contrast to later housing which faced it.*

CHAPTER 2
The Development of Houses

Just as the location and setting of a house can give clues to its age, so its layout and form can pinpoint it further. The way people have lived, their expectations, and the fashionable styles by which they could display their personal wealth have changed over the centuries. The principal rooms haven't always been on the ground floor, houses could not always be built two rooms deep and symmetry did not always control the appearance of the façade. In this chapter we look at the notable changes in the planning and style of houses and some of the common designs which might help you identify the period in which your property was built (you may wish to refer to the three labelled drawings after the introduction if you are unfamiliar with some of the parts of the house mentioned below).

THE LAYOUT OF HOUSES

The earliest houses which still stand today date from the medieval period, a few as far back as the 12th century. These exceptional and rare buildings vary depending on whether they were built of stone or timber and had to be defensive or commercial, but there are a few common designs which can be recognised. Some of the earliest are small manor houses, with a vaulted ground floor used for storage, and steps leading up the side to a first-floor hall in which the family would have lived and slept. Timber-framed halls of a similar status also survive which, although having since usually been divided up into smaller rooms, can still reveal their

Cross wings

FIG 2.1: *The basic medieval house varied in scale and grandeur rather than design. The single, rectangular space in which the occupants ate and slept was the basic component of most properties. In the manor or other important house this main unit was often expanded upon with the addition of cross wings which provided a private chamber for the owner and a service wing with buttery and pantry at the other end.*

original open form through study of the roof and main walls (soot marks might be found in the loft showing where a fire once burned in an open hall).

In the narrow burgage plots in town, the front was often used as a shop and rented out, while the open hall behind it was accessed down a side passage. On wider plots the main building could run across the front and could have been shops, a guild hall, or hostelry. In all these forms of medieval house, there would have been a series of outbuildings forming a courtyard or a line of structures down the narrow urban plot. In the larger houses the kitchen was separate due to the fire risk it posed. Most families who worked the land lived in a simple house which was no more than a single room with an adjoining byre for livestock. These were still being built well into the 18th century and in some highland districts even longer, although they rarely

FIG 2.2: *Plans of medieval urban properties arranged down a narrow burgage plot (top) or spread across a wider frontage (bottom).*

survive today. Most houses from the 12th to the 15th century which are still standing were for the better-off members of the community, and will be well recorded, with information regarding their date possibly available locally. There are, however, always surprises and every so often an old barn or humble cottage is found to have beautifully-carved trusses in the loft or thick timbers in the walls hidden beneath later cladding, thus revealing it as a medieval hall.

FIG 2.3: *A common design of large house for merchants and yeoman farmers was the Wealden house, which originated in the south-east in the late 14th century and could be found across much of the south and east in the 15th and early 16th centuries. It appears as a more compact form of the large H-shaped house with stubby cross wings and the hall under a single roof. In Yorkshire, some of these buildings were clad in stone at a later date.*

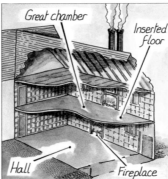

FIG 2.4: *Plan of a medieval hall (left) and in the 16th century (right) when a fireplace and floor have been inserted. Notice the blackened roof timbers in the later view.*

The first notable change in house design came about because of the widespread adoption of the fireplace and chimney. With a central fire the smoke was allowed to rise up through an opening (louvre) in the roof or was placed in a corner under a hood or bay. Once it was positioned by the wall, and the smoke ducted up through a flue, then the large open hall could be divided up horizontally to create a large first-floor room in which the owner could eat meals and entertain guests. This modification usually occurred in large houses from the late 15th century through to the 17th century, with the raising of tall and highly decorative chimney stacks characteristic of the Tudor period and a sign of status (false ones are known to have been added to make it appear you had more fireplaces than there were). The gradual separation of the lord of the manor and his household from the medieval hub of the community continued to evolve until, by the 18th century, his house was the private residence of a gentleman.

For those who chose to build from scratch, or had enjoyed an increase in wealth such that they could afford a new property, the period of the Great Rebuilding introduced a wider variety of plan and form. The largest houses often

FIG 2.5: *Defensive stone tower houses (referred to as pele towers) were common in turbulent border regions in the North and sometimes further south as in this example from Derbyshire. The late medieval tower is at the back right, the other parts are later in date, and had secure storage for livestock below the living accommodation. Two-storey bastle houses with steps or a ladder up the side were popular in the 16th and 17th centuries for lower status farmers.*

took the shape in plan of an H or an E, many with a tall central porch. Some porches were also added to existing houses where they might be in a corner over the old entrance to the screens passage. One of the most common layouts was based around a large central chimney stack, with fireplaces either side serving a living room or house place (what today we might refer to as a farmhouse kitchen) and a parlour, with bedrooms above (usually unheated) and sometimes an additional room at one end. These axial stack plans appear in the south from the mid-16th century, spreading up the country over the following hundred years although the design only seemed to be popular for a few generations in each area.

Smaller houses were often no more than two ground floor rooms, with the fireplace only in one. This simple design could be extended at a later date, with bedrooms fitted into the loft space lit by a pair of dormer windows, chimneys built in both gable ends, and

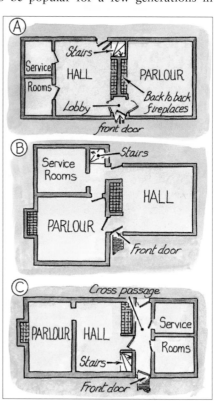

FIG 2.6: *An axial stack house as it may have originally appeared with a short lobby at the front and a staircase at the rear of the fireplaces. Many houses of this design which survive today have been changed to such a degree that it is only by the thick, square chimney (now offset to one side if extensions have been added) by which they can be recognised.*

FIG 2.7: *Plans of rural houses which could be found in the 17th century. (A) is an axial or lobby entrance type, (B) is a 'T'-shaped plan which was popular in the Midlands, and (C) is a cross passage cottage which was common in the north and west.*

FIG 2.8: *During the rebuilding of many rural estates and villages in the 18th and early 19th centuries, cottages with a central doorway, rooms either side and small bedrooms in the attic were a common plan, with the position of the chimney and staircase being the main variation between the regions. A curved protrusion at the front was the rear of a bread oven in Devon.*

a lean-to extension added along the rear (catslide roof). Another plan which was common in highland areas had two heated rooms divided by a passage, with an additional unheated room at one end. They were known as two-plus-one houses and were popular in the 17th and 18th centuries. In many long-houses, the livestock were moved out into separate outbuildings and the old byre converted into another room. The poor quality of this part of the house is still evident today when compared with the walls of the original residential half. A larger variation was for a two-storey farmhouse to have a large barn attached in line and under one roof but with a passage separating them. These laithe houses can be found in the north of the country, especially Yorkshire, and tend to date from the late 18th and early 19th centuries.

The limiting width of urban plots meant that, if you wanted to impress your neighbours and passers-by, you had to extend vertically, and narrow Tudor streets became ever darker and less than sanitary as timber-framed buildings towered ever higher, with each storey jettied over the one below. These jetties, which were rare in the country, were principally a status symbol. By the second half of the 17th century, the new building regulations banning timber and the fashion for all things Classical, led to the development of a new type of house – the brick or stone terrace. With plans copied from pattern books and short rows erected by speculative builders, they evolved with basements for the kitchen, scullery or cellars and rooms on the ground floor which could be used for professionals like lawyers and doctors rather than shops. As the hall along the side and the stairs at the rear made this floor narrow, the principal rooms for entertaining were moved to the level above (the piano nobile), with bedrooms on the upper floors and accommodation for live-in servants in the attic. By the late 18th century the ground floor began to be raised up a few feet with the front door accessed up a short flight of steps. This allowed more light and air into what is termed a half basement.

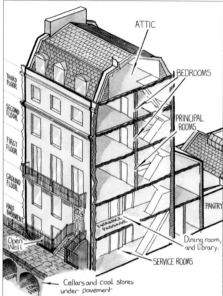

FIG 2.9: *Cut-away views of an early 18th-century terrace and a larger Regency type with a raised ground floor above a half basement. The building regulations in London divided houses into different rates depending upon the total area inside. The 1774 Act stated that those over 900 sq ft were first rate (right), 900–500 sq ft second rate (left), 500–350 sq ft third rate and under 350 sq ft was fourth rate.*

FIG 2.10: *A large urban or rural house which began to appear in the south-east from the mid-17th century and became the standard plan for detached houses of this class by 1700 in most areas. The central hallway allowed direct access to the rooms while the prominent central staircase becomes a key feature of this new plan and was imitated in 18th-century terraces where the more limited space permitted. As there was no light in this central hall, fanlights were inserted above the door.*

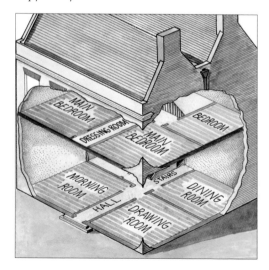

Another significant change to houses during the 17th century was that they became double piled, i.e. they were two rooms deep. Beforehand, most houses were built with just a single room depth, although they could be arranged around a courtyard or have extensions added on to appear deeper. Now changes in fashion and new solutions in roofing made it practical to build larger, stout houses with symmetrical façades – at manor house stage at first, then later in the country farmhouses. By 1700, this move had spread from the south-east and up into the Midlands. It enabled the staircase, which had formerly been tucked away in a corner, to become a key feature of the new, central hall, with beautifully-carved balustrades and newel posts making an impressive display. Positioning this entrance space in the middle also meant that, rather than having to pass through other rooms to get to the one you wanted as in single-pile houses, you could now directly access each room creating much desired privacy. In this plan the fireplaces and chimney had to be re-sited from their central position to individual ones on the end gables or in the partition walls between the front and back rooms.

In the late 18th and early 19th centuries, a new form of compact country house set in its own small garden became a feature in fashionable suburban areas. Termed a villa, its double-piled form was covered by a shallow pitched, hipped roof using the now widely available Welsh slate. A prominent overhang and fine glazed windows made them distinctive of the Regency period. During the Victorian period the term was attached to houses further down the social scale so that, by the end of the century, a row of compact terraces or semi-detached houses could be built with a dated plaque declaring themselves as villas!

FIG 2.11: *A Regency villa with its distinctive shallow pitched, hipped roof (one with the slope on all four sides). Some were semis with a lower, set back entrance linking them. Fanlights which were usually patterned semi circular types were often the only decoration on an otherwise plain stone or stucco covered façade.*

During the 19th century a number of changes were made to the plan of large detached and terraced houses. The service rooms were now either in a lighter half-basement or sited in a separate block at the rear, an improvement over most of the earlier Georgian properties. But by the later 1800s, as servants were attracted into more lucrative factory jobs, the difficulty in retaining staff meant that conditions had to improve and kitchens begin to appear in the main body or a wing of the house.

Rear extensions became a key feature of terraces during the Victorian period (rather than a later addition). At first, rather short protrusions on the largest

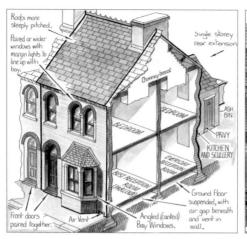

FIG 2.12: *A middle class terrace with a single storey extension from the mid 19th century (left) and one with a two-storey rear extension from around 1880s (right). The smaller working class terrace would often have a single-storey extension or separate block at the rear for a scullery by the end of the 19th century.*

FIG 2.13: *Earlier Victorian terraces had the door and chimney in the same position on each house in a row (left),. By the second half of the 19th century it was more usual for them to be paired together (right). Notice that the top windows are tight up against the roof which has little overhang on the earlier one, but in the later example there are more defined eaves and prominent lintels. Single-storey bay windows appear on this class of house from the 1860s, two-storey ones becoming common by the 1880s. The height of the building also starts increasing during the second half of the 19th century.*

terraces contained an additional staircase so that servants could move between floors without disturbing the family and guests (a further example of the gradual separation of the gentry from their household which began in the late medieval period), with service rooms on the ground floor. Later, though, houses further down the social scale gained a single storey extension in which a scullery was sited (cooking was done in the rear living room or house place, washing and laundry in the scullery), then in the late 19th century most middle class terraces had a two-storey addition with a bedroom and, in some cases, a bathroom with flushing toilet, a new feature which was popular with the middle classes but less so with the gentry who still had servants to carry water and clean out chamber pots for them!

The idea of small apartments being stacked one above another did not make an impression on the urban landscape until the later Victorian period and then often in the form of rather grim blocks of tenements to house the working classes and relieve the slums. By the turn of the 20th century new blocks of luxury flats were appearing, at first as red-brick mansions but by the 1930s, low rises in the latest art deco and modern styles. The idea of flats was discredited, however, with the 1950s and '60s boom in high-rise building – a valiant if flawed attempt to alleviate the chronic post Second World War housing crisis. At the same time many landlords were encouraged to split up their old Victorian and Georgian terraces and convert them into flats and bedsits (look for cornices and skirting boards running into walls to show where a dividing wall has been inserted).

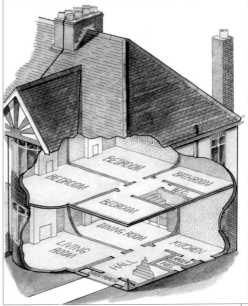

FIG 2.14: *Late Victorian and Edwardian semis usually have their doors paired in the middle with a gabled roof above (left); by the 1930s the entrances are normally on the outer side and hipped roofs were common (right). Notice also how the layout changes on the later wider plots.*

Another distinctive form of house which first appeared in the late 19th century and became something of a British institution is the bungalow (imported from Bengal, India). Its style mirrors that of a house and it tends to be a suburban feature due to the large amount of land required. The bungalow was especially common in the inter-war years. Prefabricated versions were very popular in the early 20th century, appearing in ribbon developments on the edge of towns and villages. They were often meant as temporary holiday shacks but more often than not have since been replaced by permanent brick buildings.

The most notable change in housing in the early 20th century was the development of the suburban semi. Two houses linked or built side by side with a shared party wall had been used throughout the 19th century, but now, being sited on the cheap agricultural land around towns and cities, they could expand upon larger plots with front and rear gardens, some with garages or drives down the side and a wider façade featuring curving or angled bay windows on the better-quality estates. The front doors in most 1930s semis were now on the outer side of the house rather than paired in the centre, a move which created more privacy and altered the layout inside the house. A kitchen in which washing and cooking took place was now built within the main structure, usually in the rear corner (larger houses still had a separate washroom). There was also space for a wider hallway, with the stairs brought forward so that a balustrade could be fitted and, with a small window to the side of a glazed door. There was now no need for a fanlight above the entrance which was important since ceiling heights were becoming lower.

In the 1950s, the height of the structure was further reduced, to save on material costs and reduce heating bills, and the semi in this austere period is generally stripped of ornamentation with bay windows (if they were fitted) being just simple angled types. This period also saw the introduction of open-plan interiors, not so much a reflection of a fashion amongst architects and designers for all things modern, but to enable them to make houses and flats smaller without appearing cramped. As the cost of land and building has escalated in the last fifty years so this limitation on space has remained with us, making older houses with large plots or tall ceilings an attractive proposition.

STYLES OF HOUSES

The style of a façade was of little concern to most medieval carpenters and masons. The arrangement and use of rooms determined the exterior appearance, the only concession being the tracery in windows (the patterns formed by the divisions within the opening) of the finest stone houses or the decorative timber work inserted between the structural framework. By the Tudor period, the effects of the Renaissance on the continent began to permeate through to the gentry here and, in the second half of the 16th century, large houses inspired by buildings from Ancient Rome began to be erected in this new Classical style. For the first time the outward appearance began to control the interior of houses as these new buildings had

Decorative framing   Entrance porch   Bay window   Square framing

FIG 2.15: *The ideas of symmetry began influencing housing at a manor and farmhouse level but usually only in a roughly balanced façade sometimes with a central porch or, as on this 16th-century house, with one over the entrance to the screens passage at the lower end of the hall (mirrored by the bay at the high end).*

symmetrical façades. But the designers had little understanding of the rules on proportion and the orders, so these early Classical houses tend to have decorative elements sometimes crudely stacked upon each other.

More modest urban and rural houses were still being built with a timber frame, and the style of decoration varied through the regions. The house was designed to impress visitors with the quantity of decorative elements rather than the refinement of the façade. Vertical pieces of wood fitted tightly together along one or more storeys (close studding) was a common form originating in the wealthy wool districts in the east and spreading across the country in the 16th and early 17th centuries, while decorative framing with pieces of timber cut to form patterns and shapes within a small square frame was popular in northern and western districts.

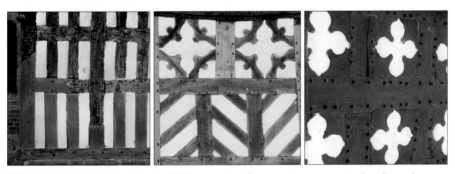

FIG 2.16: *In the 16th and early 17th centuries the most important timber-framed houses could have close studding (left) or decorative framing (centre and right), the latter principally found in the north and west. In the east, pargetting (decorative plasterwork) covering the frame was popular although most which survives today dates from the last century. The exterior may also have been brightly coloured in the past, the familiar black and white scheme only becoming widespread in the Victorian period.*

FIG 2.17: *A late 17th-century house (top left) with cross windows, hooded doorway and gabled dormers which were popular in the northern and western counties (Dutch gables were popular in eastern counties at the same time) and a slightly later one in a Dutch style with prominent white cornice and dormers (top right). By the 1720s the most up-to-date houses now had parapets, arched lintels, sash windows and prominent decorative rainwater traps (bottom right).*

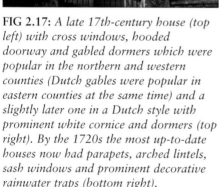

Classical architecture imported from the Low Countries began to influence house design in the second half of the 17th century. They were refined, stout, double-piled houses, with raised corner-stones (quoins) and a prominent white cornice below a hipped roof, featuring a row of dormer windows and they were popular with the gentry. On the next step down the social scale, brick and stone replaced timber-framing, and double-piled, symmetrically-fronted, three to five bays wide houses were a common sight by the turn of the 18th century. Small horizontal windows of the past were now replaced by tall rectangular openings, at first with a stone cross holding leaded glass then, by 1700, with new sliding sash windows (see Chapter 4). On Tudor houses rain had been kept off windows by a protruding lip around each opening called a hood mould, now this was replaced by a horizontal band marking each floor level called a string mould. Although the façade was becoming rather plain in the late 17th and early 18th centuries, a large semi-circular hood with a convex underside and often shell-like plasterwork was a distinctive feature above the front door.

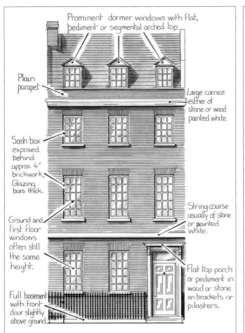

Prominent dormer windows with flat, pediment or segmental arched top.

Plain parapet

Large cornice either of stone or wood painted white.

Sash box exposed behind approx 4" brickwork. Glazing bars thick.

String course usually of stone or painted white.

Ground and first floor windows often still the same height.

Full basement with front door slightly above ground.

Flat top porch or pediment in wood or stone on brackets or pilasters.

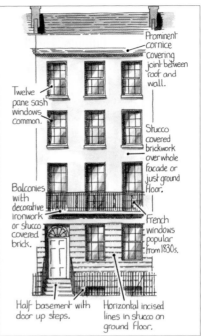

Prominent cornice covering joint between roof and wall.

Twelve pane sash windows common.

Stucco covered brickwork over whole facade or just ground floor.

Balconies with decorative ironwork or stucco covered brick.

French windows popular from 1830s.

Half basement with door up steps.

Horizontal incised lines in stucco on ground floor.

FIG 2.18: *An early (left) and a late (right) Georgian terrace with labels of their distinctive features.*

FIG 2.19: *The Ancient orders were based upon the proportions of the plinth, column and entablature of temples but are most easily recognised by the style of capital. The Roman types of Doric (left) and Corinthian (centre left) were popular throughout most of the 18th century; the plainer Greek versions of Doric (centre right) and Ionic (right) were distinctive of the early 19th century. These could feature at the top of columns or on pilasters (flat columns built into the wall).*

FIG 2.20: *Despite the dominance of foreign styles there was one home-grown source of inspiration which influenced houses in the later part of the 18th century, the Gothick (with a 'k' to differentiate it from the more correct later forms). It was a rather playful style using forms and decoration seen on medieval buildings and appeared at first on whimsical estate buildings but was more widely used on urban housing in the Regency period. Windows with hood moulds, wide pointed arches and 'Y' shaped tracery, stuccoed exteriors, gable ends with battlements and prominent chimneys were distinctive. Another variation popular for estate buildings was Cottage Orne with distinctive low thatched roofs over round, square and polygonal structures.*

The 18th-century house style is dominated by Classical architecture. The Baroque (a term coined as an insult by a later generation meaning mis-shaped shell) had a monumental scale and exuberant decoration which did not translate well onto smaller properties other than in the adoption of its proportions on some façades and parapets with the odd vase in a corner. The Palladian-style which emerged in the 1720s was more influential (named after the 16th-century architect Andreas Palladio who produced books with his designs based upon the buildings of Ancient Rome). Its refined appearance, stripped of unnecessary decoration (which suited the new building regulations which were removing any timber work from the front), and with an emphasis upon correct application of the orders and proportions, shaped the finest country houses and urban terraces in the middle of the century. In the second half of the 1700s new designs based upon the latest studies of Ancient Greek architecture began to influence houses, at first in the hands of the Adams brothers, with less austere façades broken perhaps by a band or roundels containing delicate, shallow decoration and then, later, by a more severe Neo-Classical form.

FIG 2.21: *The Neo-Classical style of the early 19th century was more severe and austere than other Regency styles. Wide arches across the façade (right), and shallow broken pediments on a gable end (left) were some of the distinctive features of these early 19th-century houses.*

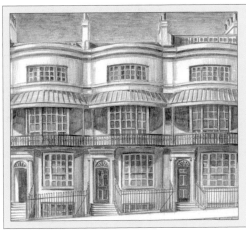

FIG 2.22: *Regency houses are distinguished by decorative iron work and shallow bow windows (although these could be applied to older buildings). Many of the finest rows of terraces were treated as a whole to appear like a country house, so they have a central pedimented feature and the end houses brought forward. They also liked to let the outside in so French doors or tall sashes front and back were often fitted.*

Terracotta finials and ridge tiles

Patterns formed in the roof tiles

Large single panes of glass

Glass upper panels in door

Outward facing gables and bargeboards

Terracotta mouldings

Deeply recessed doorways with tiled sides and floor.

Bay windows now popular on smaller houses.

FIG 2.23: *An 1870s' Gothic terrace, with labels.*

In the Regency period of the early 19th century a much wider range of styles developed which was inspired by a growing awareness of our own historic buildings, trade contact with the Far East and Napoleon's study of Ancient Egypt. The Gothick, Chinese and Egyptian styles, however, tended to be decoration applied to a still mainly classically-proportioned structure with a symmetrical façade. The mass production of iron meant that features like balconies, window guards and porches, with intricate decoration and pagoda-type roofs, became a common addition to terraces and the newly-popular villa; while shallow bow windows were a luxurious addition popular in seaside and spa resorts. The pedimented or semi-circular arched entrance began to be replaced by rectangular openings with a flat-roofed portico (a porch supported on columns) protruding from the front, now proudly standing at the top of a short flight of stairs.

The accession of Queen Victoria to the throne in 1838 came at a time when a

FIG 2.24: *An Italianate-style house, with its distinctive round arched windows, deep eaves supported on brackets or stepped brickwork and shallow slate roofs.*

battle of styles began to rage between those who promoted the Classical and those who believed that a home-grown style based upon medieval architecture was more appropriate. By the 1850s and '60s this new Gothic style began to dominate domestic building. Larger houses could now have asymmetrical designs with gable ends, towers and offset entrances breaking the formerly balanced façade. Brick was back on show and stucco discredited partly on ethical grounds which promoted honesty in architecture but also because it had become associated with poor-quality construction and cheap materials. Roofs began to be raised in pitch on fashionable houses and covered with slate and, later, clay tiles. A problem on many ordinary houses was the pointed arch, the key component of Gothic architecture, which had to fit in with the rectangular sash window. Some were made to fit behind an arch while others had an impression of it made in the brickwork above. With the classical parapet gone, the chimney returned to

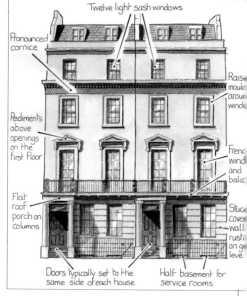

Twelve light sash windows

Pronounced cornice

Raise mould arou wind

Pediments above openings on the first floor

Frenc wind and balc

Flat roof porch on columns

Stucc cover wall rush on g leve

Doors typically set to the same side of each house

Half basement for service rooms

FIG 2.25: *A mid Victorian Classical-style terrace from London still covered in stucco but differing from earlier types (see Fig 2.18), with the raised moulding around the windows and a square fanlight and portico over the front door. They are less refined and more muscular than Georgian types.*

Tall chimneys.

Long, low slung roofs

Prominent gables to the front.

Elongated, low windows.

Staggered sides of window frames.

Mullioned windows.

Mix of materials (Stone and Timber)

FIG 2.26: *A revival of domestic styles from the late 16th and 17th centuries was popular in the 1880s and 1890s. They could range from rambling country residences which hid amongst the landscape to modest urban houses, most with timber-framed upper storeys (or cladding) above a stone or brick ground floor (original timber-framed structures rested upon the ground). Today houses like this example are often labelled Arts and Crafts.*

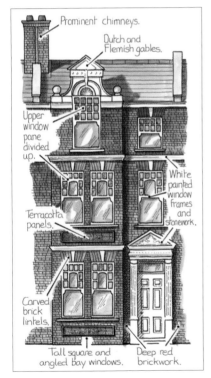

Prominent chimneys.

Dutch and Flemish gables.

Upper window pane divided up.

White painted window frames and stonework.

Terracotta panels.

Carved brick lintels.

Tall square and angled bay windows.

Deep red brickwork.

FIG 2.27: *A Queen Anne-style house from the 1880s, with labels of its key features (see also Fig 1.10).*

the fore: plain brick on most but on some given an Elizabethan or Tudor theme; tall octagonal or twisted brick types were revived.

The Classical style remained popular in some cities and a variation referred to as Italianate was very popular after it was used on Victoria and Albert's Osborne House on the Isle of Wight and was widely copied on middle-class terraces. Shallow pitched slate roofs with deep eaves and brackets, towers with groups of narrow openings, and round-arched windows often set in pairs were popular in the 1850s and '60s. Those Classical terraces which were still being built in this period were similar to their Regency counterparts but with raised mouldings around the windows and more prominent cornices as the Victorians' love of decoration enlivened the façade. Balconies fell from favour and houses began to be set back from the road as families sought greater privacy, a move copied on middle-class housing later in the century. Angled bay windows were preferred to Regency bows, especially after window tax was repealed in 1851 and they

FIG 2.28: *The Orchards by C.F.A. Voysey is one of the finest Arts and Crafts houses in which traditional buildings inspired new forms.*

became cheaper, such that middle-class terraces in the 1860s and '70s could afford a single-storey addition and, by the final decades of the century, a square or angled bay running up the full height of the house was common.

In the late Victorian period there was a reaction against the strict medieval Gothic and a new generation of architects sought inspiration from rustic manor houses and timber-framed farm buildings to create distinctive new forms which today are banded together under the Arts and Crafts banner. The first of these domestic revivals used black and white timber-framed structures (or just a cladding) raised above a brick or stone ground floor with distinctive tall Tudor-style chimneys and leaded light windows. Another style was the Queen Anne which was popular in the 1880s and '90s with rich red-brick walls and white-painted woodwork (most window frames and doors previously had been painted in dark colours or grained to appear like wood) and the use of Dutch gables, fine-cut brickwork and terracotta mouldings and plaques. In the 1890s and early 1900s some of the leading architects inspired by the Arts and Crafts movement designed new houses which seemed almost modern in form yet vernacular in source. Low-slung roofs, long rows of mullioned windows, steep-angled buttresses, and walls

FIG 2.29: *In the 1890s and early 1900s, houses reached a pinnacle of quality and size. Features borrowed from Queen Anne and Arts and Crafts-style houses were used to decorate middle class terraces now set back behind a small walled garden, with chimneys characteristically built halfway down the pitch of the roof. White-painted woodwork around the door and along small balconies, stained glass in the upper pane of casement windows which now began replacing the traditional sash were distinctive of this period.*

covered in hanging tiles or pebbledash were introduced by them and widely copied in the early decades of the 20th century.

After the First World War the standard house structure, now more often semi-detached, could be decorated in a number of different styles. The Neo-Georgian which reflected a revival in Classical architecture in the Edwardian period was popular in the 1920s but fell from favour as it became widely adopted on council housing. Façades were symmetrical, with brick walls, tiled hipped roofs, small leaded casement windows and hoods or pediments above the door. A Tudor or Olde English style was very popular with mock timber-framed gables, herringbone brickwork and dark wood doors, with vertical strips and black iron work. For the more daring streamline Moderne style, a watered down version of contemporary Continental and American styles (today generally referred to as Art Deco) was favoured, with white rendered walls, distinctive curved steel-framed windows, plain horizontal bands and prominent zigzag or chevron-shaped patterns. On many estates, a mixture of features from these and the still influential Arts and Crafts style could make a pleasing façade.

FIG 2.30: *Three examples of the different styles which could be found in the 1920s and 1930s: Neo Georgian (top left) was inspired by late 17th- and early 18th-century houses (ironically before the Georgian period) and differed from the originals by larger, sharp edged bricks and squatter sash or casement windows. Tudor or Olde English (bottom left) borrowed heavily from Arts and Crafts-style houses while the Streamlined Moderne (bottom right) was a watered down version of the International and Moderne styles.*

CHAPTER 3
Materials and Construction

The materials used and the methods of construction can help date part or the whole of a building. The size of a brick, the joints in a timber frame, the finish of masonry and the way the walls have been built all provide clues since they changed depending on fashion, regulations and improved transportation. Before improvements to rivers, roads and the emergence of canals in the 18th century, most materials had to be sourced locally since only the wealthy could afford the costs of transporting heavy loads. The mass production of bricks, improved quarrying techniques, imports of timber and the availability of decorative pieces through catalogues during the 19th century brought down the cost of building. At the same time, though, it ended the link between the house and its immediate landscape. In this chapter we look at these factors from the foundations up to the roof and the details which can narrow down when they were built.

FOUNDATIONS

Despite the belief that the quality of older houses is superior to that of modern houses, the foundations of most pre-20th-century houses are dramatically shallow compared to today's, and have only stood the test of time due to the flexibility of their timber framework or the lime mortar between bricks and stones. Many houses had only the soft earth removed before walls were erected. It was not until the Georgian period that it became common for large terraces to have stone slabs inserted beneath to help spread the load. Bricks were stepped out by the Victorians for the same effect, with concrete footings being introduced from the late 19th century (see Fig 3.1).

Unless there is building work taking place which permits access to them, the

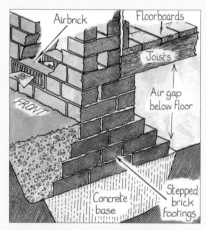

FIG 3.1: *Details of the foundations of an Edwardian house, with air bricks venting under the floorboards to reduce damp.*

foundations of the house will not directly shed much light on a house's history; however, there are other details which might. Preventing damp rising up within walls was first tackled in the second half of the 19th century when damp-proof courses were first introduced, usually no more than a thin course of slate or bitumen near the base or a line of grey engineering bricks. At the same time, the ground floor was raised a few feet above the soil and vents fitted in the wall so that air could pass beneath the floorboards keeping them dry (see Fig 3.1). Houses where this has been done usually date from the 1870s to the 1930s.

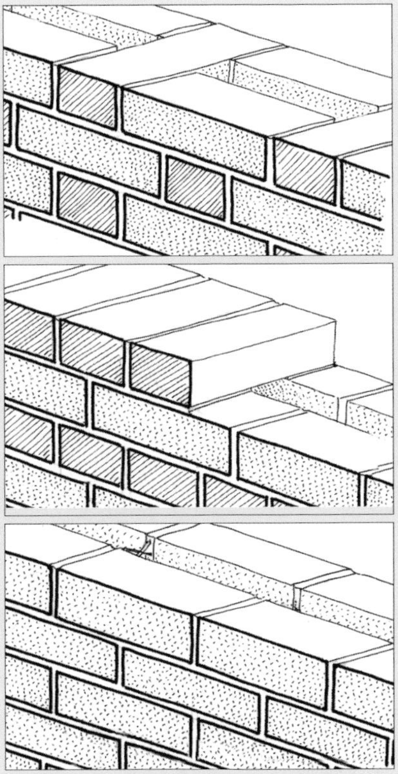

Any room below the ground can be worth inspecting. It might be a survivor from an earlier house and it is not uncommon to find a brick structure built on an earlier stone vaulted cellar (one with a ceiling formed from arched brickwork or stonework). In most cases, the only clue to identifying if the cellar is older than the house above is by studying the brick or stonework for dating clues. Full-depth basements were common in early Georgian houses for the service rooms; half-basements with steps leading up to the door are more usual in the Regency period and were out of fashion by the late Victorian (although basements can be found from all periods where the land slopes).

FIG 3.2: *Georgian and Victorian 9in walls were virtually solid (Flemish bond top, English bond centre) but cavity walls first used in some coastal areas like Southampton from the 1860s were standard elsewhere by the 1920s. These can be identified by the use of stretcher bond on the outer skin (bottom).*

WALLS

Walls serve two principal roles in a house: firstly to support the roof and upper floors and secondly to keep the interior warm and dry. It is the first role which determines the thickness and nature of the wall as the weight and pitch of the roof will try and force the structure outwards. Imagine two playing cards resting against each other like a roof and how their bottom edges slip outwards when the angle between them gets too shallow. It is worth bearing this role in mind when looking at the structure and the, sometimes, complex arrangement of timbers in the roof space. Walls were usually solid before the turn of the 20th century; after the First World War it became common for a cavity to be formed between an inner brick or breeze-block wall and the outer skin (it is the inside one which takes the load and the outer which is only for weather-proofing and appearance) with metal ties holding the two together.

STONE

In the medieval and early Tudor period, masons were concentrated in cities and ecclesiastical centres where there was always work to be found. Away from these regions, there would be limited quality stone building work, except for the houses of the wealthy and the parish church. Where suitable stone could be found a small quarry might open for a single large project or small pits dug to provide rough pieces to make rubble walls for lesser buildings (these excavations often survive around villages). In some cases pieces of masonry could have been taken from a disused building like a castle or old house, although the owner of the land was likely to reuse this for any replacement structure. After the Dissolution of the Monasteries in the 1530s, materials were sold off and often used in any building that might appear on the site of an abbey. From the late 16th century, as church building dried up and wealth became more widely dispersed, masons became established in towns and cities. In the following century, as permanent quarries opened up, smaller, quality stone houses became common in areas such as the Cotswolds, although in some poorer highland regions they may not have appeared until the late Georgian period. By this time, precisely-cut blocks with fine joints (ashlar) was the most fashionable material to use; imitating it with stucco was the answer for those who could not afford it or could not get supplies. The Gothic revival made brick fashionable again and it could be even

FIG 3.3: *Flints (right), cobbles and pebbles (left) have also been used in the past to make walls in areas with poor stone, mainly in East Anglia and over the Chilterns and the Downs. They usually form rough rubble walls set in mortar but need stone or, more usually, brick to form the corners, a course between floors and dressing around openings. As these materials have still been used in modern times (albeit as a facing rather than for structural purposes), dating is tricky although the nature of the bricks used should help and you would expect older buildings to have thicker and more uneven walls. Pebbles are usually only found on houses less than 200 years old.*

seen in areas where the still more expensive stone was readily available. There are towns in the north and west where Victorian stone terraces were still common; in other areas it is likely to have been used for dressing (squared off corner stones, mouldings, lintels and sills).

Stone walls are rarely composed of finely squared-off blocks all the way through. Most will have a layer of these (or even thinner facing stones) across the main façade with rougher and, hence, cheaper blocks or bricks behind it and also down the sides and rear; a pre-industrial age house with ashlar all the way around would constitute a notable building within the neighbourhood. Sometimes stones were only roughly squared off and set in courses to create solid but less refined walls. Most cheaper housing before the mid 19th century had them made from rubble (rough stones not laid in neat

FIG 3.4: *Dating stone walls is tricky. It will be best to look at similar buildings of known date in the area first, noting the use of the same types, size of blocks, and the way they have been finished to help narrow down when yours was built. Badly worn stone can imply age but some stones wear faster than others or could have been reused while older blocks have often been re-cut or pointed so it is easy to be misled. There were fashions, however, in the finish of blocks: the Georgians liked smooth, finely cut walls (left) while the Victorians reacted against this in the second half of the 19th century with raised naturalistic stonework (right). Note the brickwork behind what is often just an outer skin of stone in the left-hand view.*

FIG 3.5: *As stone decorative pieces were always expensive, builders often used other materials like stucco, plaster and, later, terracotta as a substitute. However, the most convincing alternative was an artificial material called Coade stone, invented in 1767 by George and Eleanor Coade. It was a type of ceramic with quartz, glass and flint mixed with a special clay from the south-west and fired at a consistent high temperature for up to four days (a very skilled job in those days). The finished product was a very durable matt grey/beige material which was moulded to form keystones (above), decorative details and plaques until the 1840s (it is more common in London where the Coades were based).*

horizontal lines), usually with larger blocks at the bottom and smaller ones towards the top. However, these random rubble walls required cross pieces running through for stability (these through stones often project out from the face in some highland areas). It is also worth noting marks on stonework: a mason's mark was a crude signature which would identify the builder of the wall. You might find matching marks on other buildings in the area of known date. Semi-circular grooves found on the edge of some stones were made when charges were being drilled into the rock: they will be of late 18th-century date at the earliest.

BRICKS

As a manufactured product, bricks are much easier to date than other materials, with their size, finish and method of laying them in a wall changing throughout the centuries. The Romans first brought bricks to these shores: flat almost tile-like pieces which, although reused by later Saxon and Norman builders, had generally been exhausted as a supply by the 13th century. Around the same time, Flemish immigrants (from Flanders, now part of Belgium) started to settle in East Anglia and began producing bricks. Their skills spread so that by the 16th century it was a luxury product used mainly in the eastern and southern counties. Bricks appeared in the Midlands during the 17th century and then up into parts of the north, not making an impact in the Pennine region until the mid 19th century. It was only later in each region that they were used on lesser dwellings although the widespread establishment of local brickworks meant that by the early 1800s it was a common material for most sizes of house. (Before this time bricks were often made on site from clay dug from within the plot or surrounding land.)

FIG 3.6: *The date at which brick replaced stone as the common building material in a local area can be useful for dating houses. Look in local books covering architecture like Pevsner's* Buildings of England *series (see Chapter 6). In Leek it occurred in the late 18th century and despite the good local sources of stone (right) most Regency houses in the town are of brick (left).*

The earliest bricks tended to vary greatly in size from great bricks which were 12 inches x 6 inches (although not designed for ordinary houses) down to smaller Flemish bricks which could vary from 8–9 inches x 4–4½ inches (bricks tend to be slightly larger in the north than the south). In 1571, regulations were introduced to control the dimensions, and

FIG 3.7: *Early bricks were flat (left) but from around the turn of the 19th century, indentations in the top and bottom of bricks called frogs were introduced. If you can get access to one, then look for the name of the brick company as you may be able to date it from its form or from the records of the firm which could be held in local or county record offices. These examples are from an excellent display of brick-making at Avoncroft Museum of Historic Buildings in Bromsgrove, Worcs. (Similar information is at the Weald and Downland Open Air Museum, Singleton, Sussex.)*

a statute brick was introduced at 9 x 4½ x 2¼ inches. The size has remaining pretty consistent, except in the final figure: the thickness. Most bricks were only 2 inches thick before 1600, 2½ inches up to the early 18th century, and then generally 2¾ –3 inches. The introduction of the Brick Tax in 1784 was designed to bring in revenue after the disastrous American War of Independence, and was calculated upon the quantity used. Manufacturers simply made them larger to reduce the amount due until they later returned to a more standard size.

The way that bricks are laid to form a wall (the bonding) has also changed over the centuries. Before the 17th century there was little clear pattern and walls were often built quite thick (1½ brick lengths, about 14 inches). The earliest regular form

FIG 3.8: *Examples of brick bonding from right to left: English bond (early 17th-century bricks), Flemish bond (late 18th-century with thin lines of lime putty inserted to make it look like fine brickwork called tuck pointing), Stretcher bond (late 19th-century Accrington reds, extremely tough surface which hardly wears). The final example is of English Garden Wall bond where an extra couple of rows of stretchers are inserted between that of headers(can also be done to Flemish bond). Note the difference in size of the bricks; the lower examples date from the late 18th century to reduce brick tax.*

FIG 3.9: *It has been fashionable at certain times to use different coloured bricks to form patterns within a wall. Diapur patterns using over burnt grey ends of bricks to form diamonds and similar geometric shapes in red-brick walls were common in the 16th and early 17th centuries (left). The headers of Flemish bond were often a contrasting colour in the early 19th century (centre) while in the 1860s and 1870s polychromic brickwork was popular, usually mixes of red, yellow and dark grey bricks (right).*

was English Bond in which a course of headers (the short end exposed so the brick is laying across the width of the wall), then a layer of stretchers (the long side exposed), which was popular during the 17th century (this was reintroduced in the late 19th-century revival of traditional styles). Flemish Bond, in which each course has alternate headers and stretchers along it, was dominant during the 18th and 19th centuries. Header bond was widely used on curved bay and bow windows as continuous rows of short exposed ends could form a smooth radius. With the widespread adoption of cavity walls from the early 20th century, stretcher bond became standard since a facing comprised completely of stretchers will leave a void behind it; steel ties are set in the mortar and used to tie into the inner load-bearing skin.

There have been many variations on these patterns. One of the most common is to introduce three or more courses of stretchers between each row of headers. This cheaper and weaker walling is often referred to as 'garden wall' since that is where it was often used. Rat Trap Bond was devised to reduce the amount payable under the Brick Tax and was used on cheaper properties, with the bricks set on their thinner side and the wider base facing out. This meant that fewer bricks were used but the wall was more fragile and prone to getting damp in the gaps created within. The thickness of mortar also varies. Early walls had thick beds due to the uneven bricks, with this narrowing down to between ¼ inch and ½ inch during the 17th century. In some of the best work in Georgian and Victorian houses, it was so fine as to appear little more than a thin line. Softer red bricks could also be cut and sanded down to make the precise shapes required to form arches and decorative details.

TIMBER

Timber has been used to form the structure of houses from prehistoric times right up to modern housing estates where many seemingly brick houses have a wooden framework holding them up. Whereas the Romans used timber framing (where a grid of vertical and horizontal pieces were joined and the gaps between infilled with another material), the Saxons, for many of their buildings, reverted to solid walls with vertical posts strapped together. Timber framing was revived during the medieval period with two principal forms:

- cruck construction – where a slightly bent tree was split down the middle to make two matching bowed trunks which could form a pointed arch frame linked to the next by horizontal pieces; and
- box framing – where a rectangular framework formed the main structure.

Cruck framing was popular in the north and west of the country but fell from favour by the 16th century when a variety of forms of box framing became dominant. Timber framing died out after the mid-17th century, very quickly in urban areas due to building regulations but continued to be used in the country well into the 18th century. It was revived in the 1870s, although usually only for the upper floors and in many cases only a thin cladding was applied to a stone or brick structure.

The medieval timber-framed houses which survive today tend to have thick lengths of timber of an irregular shape; Tudor timber tends to be straighter; while late 17th- and 18th-century examples are notably thinner as they tended to be used on more humble cottages. The later houses might also contain a few substantial timbers taken from old houses. To hide these less substantial frames, many were covered with weatherboarding (mainly in the south-east) or with hanging tiles. Originally, the pieces would have been connected by a joint formed out of the ends or cut into a side, each one designed to resist a certain load and held together by

FIG 3.10: *Examples of medieval framing with thick pieces of timber and large panels (left), a crucks frame with its distinctive inverted 'V' timbers (centre) and Tudor small square framing with panels varying from 1 to 2 feet across (right).*

wooden pegs, although in the 18th century iron bolts and straps were commonly used. Look out for peg holes and sockets in beams which may show where a partition wall has been removed or that the timber has been resited from somewhere else (see Fig 5.2). As timber-framed houses were often cut, jointed and partially assembled in a yard before being taken to site and erected in place, carpenters made simple marks (usually Roman numerals or similar symbols) either side of joints so they would know which one went where, and if they are found today they can be useful in confirming whether or not the piece is still in its original location.

The infill of the panels within the frame was traditionally done with wattle and daub, the former being a mesh of vertical sticks and horizontal weave, the latter a mix of clay, straw and other local ingredients which were applied over it. The underside of the top bar had small holes in it to receive the vertical staves, the lower one had a slot into which they were inserted. These details can be found after later infill is removed or if a piece of timber has been resited. Brick was sometimes used in the 16th and early 17th centuries on the finer timber-framed house: they would be distinctive thinner bricks often set in a herringbone (diagonal) pattern. In the following centuries, as bricks became cheaper, they were used as a maintenance-free replacement for wattle and daub (although they actually cause more problems than they solve) and will usually be laid in horizontal courses and be of regular statute size.

FIG 3.11: *Fake timber framing was popular in the late 19th and early 20th centuries but usually can be told apart from the genuine article as in the above views (original top, cladding bottom). Later imitations are usually a cheaper painted wood, have sharp edges, pegs standing proud of the planks, and marks from machine cutting (vertical bands on the lower example). Original timber-framed houses were usually built on the ground while Victorian imitations had a ground floor in brick or stone (some old houses had the lower storey encased in stone or brick at a later date so they can look like Victorian ones although the material should appear older than the 19th century).*

As timber framing fell from fashion in the 17th century, so those who could not afford to replace the complete structure used other ways of making their house appear more up-to-date. Some were rendered all over, some were encased in brick or stone, and sometimes just the façade was done (so its original form will still be visible to the rear). At other times the whole house was covered with brick or stone, as with many farmhouses and halls in the Pennines and Yorkshire. In some cases jettied houses had the upper

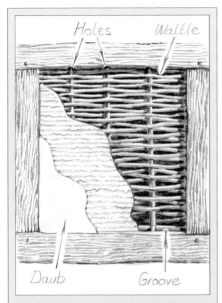

FIG 3.12: *A panel of wattle and daub with the frame exposed so you can see the slot at the bottom and holes at the top, features you might spot on timbers today in situ or reused elsewhere.*

floor covered with hanging tiles and a brick wall inserted below so the original lower wall could be removed, making a slightly larger ground floor area. Oak or elm weatherboarding had been used mainly on agricultural buildings and coastal properties in the past but, during the Georgian period, softwood painted white was used to cover up poorly-built houses or older buildings, and became popular in Kent and Sussex in the 19th century. Earlier weatherboarding was pegged to the frame, later more regular boards were nailed.

It was common for sash windows to be inserted on the façade. Where you find them today in less than perfect symmetry or appearing to sag, it could mean there is a timber frame behind (although dubious Georgian building can also be to blame). A clever solution, employed mainly in the south-east, was to use mathematical tiles which, when carefully hung across the façade, looked just like bricks. They date from the mid-18th century and were popular through to the 19th century (the

FIG 3.13: *Hanging tiles were a popular way of covering up a timber frame on upper storeys, first appearing in Kent and Sussex during the late 17th century and were especially popular on poorer housing in the late 18th century. Weatherboarding was used in a similar way to disguise old or poor quality frames. Slates were also used, especially in Cumbria, Wales and Devon, and like the other forms could also be used to protect vulnerable walls or to modernise the appearance. Mathematical tiles were used in the late 18th and early 19th centuries to make the façade appear to be of brick (you can usually tell it at the corners where a vertical strip was applied).*

FIG 3.14: *Timber-framed buildings often had a brick or stone façade added in the 18th century to make them appear more up to date. Sagging windows which do not line up horizontally, exposed timber at the side or rear and a steep pitched roof designed originally for thatch but now hidden behind a later parapet are all clues to where this has happened.*

Brick Tax did not affect them), and it is often only at the corners, where a strip was used to cover the junction, that it can be spotted.

COB OR WITCHERT

Mud walls were a traditional type of construction now limited to certain areas, notably Devon and neighbouring areas, where it is known as cob, and north Buckinghamshire where it is called witchert. The clay or mud has straw and sometimes gravel, sand, pebbles, broken slate, brick or even crockery added, all bound together with animal dung. The mixture is then built up in slab-like layers upon a dwarf wall of rubble to keep it away from damp. The outer surface was then whitewashed or rendered with tar applied around the base. This form can be distinguished by its rounded corners, small deep-set doors and windows, and a base which is usually wider than the top of the wall. Most date from the late 18th and early 19th centuries, although some may be a bit older, proving them to be surprisingly durable as long as the roof (which should have deeply overhanging eaves to keep the rain off the walls) and the base are maintained. In some parts of Norfolk and the New Forest this mixture was formed into bricks or rammed into wooden shuttering and used to make workers' cottages – mainly in the 19th century.

RENDER

At various times, and for either protection or fashion, all types of wall have been covered up by rendering clay, plaster or cement mixes. Early types were probably no more than clay, straw and dung thrown at walls to weatherproof them. From the late 16th century it became fashionable to apply lime plaster built up over horizontal laths (thin strips of wood nailed to the house). This surface could be decorated with raised patterns or scoured and combed designs known as pargeting (from 'par' meaning all over and 'jeter" to throw) and was popular, especially in East Anglia, during the 17th and early 18th centuries. Most pargeting you can still see today, however, dates from the revival of the art in the late 19th and 20th centuries.

FIG 3.15: *Most medieval and some later buildings were lime-washed, (ground chalk or kilned lime mixed with skimmed milk or tallow as a binder) some with colours added. Ochres, dark reds, and pinks were used in certain regions; bright yellows, blues and greens were only introduced in the 18th and 19th centuries. The example in this view from Suffolk has an area of pargetting, which could be formed by building up a raised design or stamping a pattern into the plaster. Most examples today date from the past 150 years, although there are some older pieces with deep raised patterns.*

Stucco is a term applied to smooth renders which were popular in the 18th and 19th centuries. (The Italian architect Andreo Palladio recommended it to cover up the joints and texture in a wall which might distract the eye from appreciating the building's form.) Originally lime plaster was used but cements introduced from the late 18th century replaced it. Some such as Portland cement were popular because they dried to the colour of Portland stone which was fashionable at the time; others had to be painted to match them (white was never used and is a 20th-century fashion). In the late 19th century, Arts and Crafts architects revived rendering, usually using roughcast which had small pieces of aggregate mixed in or pebbledash in which larger stones were thrown at the wet render. These finishes remained popular for the first floor level in suburban houses into the 1930s.

ROOFS

The form and angle of the slope of a roof varied through the centuries depending upon the weight of the covering and its ability to shed rainwater. They are also prone to being updated, often where a cheaper lightweight material might replace thatch or to enable a room to be fitted into the loft space. Most early houses had gabled roofs, i.e. with the roof running the full width or length of the house and ending with a triangular top to the wall (the gable) at each end. Hipped roofs have a slope on all four sides and do not require a gable. They are harder to construct and were found on some of the finer rural properties in the 16th and 17th centuries. Low pitched slate versions were popular in the Regency period and steeper versions became distinctive on inter-war semis. Mansard roofs have a very steep slope immediately above the wall and then a shallow one up to the ridge; this enabled a room to be fitted in the loft space and was very popular on large terraced properties from the 18th century onwards. Some roofs have a more shallow pitched lower section designed to throw the rainwater further away from the wall before gutters

FIG 3.16: *One of the biggest problems facing builders was how to span a double piled house. In the late 17th and early 18th centuries one popular solution was a double roof with a central gulley down the middle (see FIG 2.10). The widespread availability of lighter slates from the late 18th century meant houses could now be covered with a shallow pitched hipped roof (centre) but many terraces had the slope running up to the dividing walls (which were extended upwards to prevent fire spreading) from a central gulley (left) or had mansard roofs (right). Steep pitched roofs came back into fashion in the mid-19th century.*

became common in the 18th century, although it was also used for stylistic reasons in more recent centuries.

Thatch

Thatch was the most widespread roof covering in the medieval and Tudor period, only falling from favour in the 17th century due to the fire risk. It remained popular in rural areas until the early 19th century (when the introduction of threshing machines made the straw useless for roofing, and slate and clay tiles became widely available). Due to its rough surface, rainwater does not shed quickly over thatch so it is always set at a steep pitch of 45° – 60° so that gravity can help to speed it on its way; there is usually a deep overhang so it is thrown clear of the wall below. The finest thatch is made from Norfolk reeds and can last generations before it needs to be completely replaced. Long straw needs attention more regularly although often only the top decayed layer is renewed. In theory, therefore, it can be possible to find the underside preserved from when there was an open fire in the house, with blackening still evident.

It was also common for a ring of bricks, stones or mortar to be fitted around the base of the chimney just above the thatch to stop water flowing down its side and through the roof (flashing) and these often survive where the roof has since been changed. In many areas it was common for the gable ends to be extended up to form a short parapet which could protect the vulnerable ends of the thatch from wind and rain damage. Where there is a different covering today, and the pitch is very steep, this can be a sign that the roof may have once been thatched, but they were also used in many highland areas whatever the material so it is not conclusive.

Slates

Some sandstones and limestones can be split to form thick slates suitable to cover roofs and are distinctive in areas like the Cotswolds and the Pennines. They vary in size up to 3 or 4 ft wide although the larger, thicker and, hence, heavier slabs are positioned directly above the wall graduating up to the smallest ones at the top ridge. The pitch can be as shallow as 30° although 40–50° is more common. Metamorphic slates from Wales, Cornwall and the Lake District were much lighter and, with their smooth surface, shed water with ease so when they became widely available (as transport improved from the late 18th century) they were very popular on new houses and to replace old coverings.

Clay Tiles

Clay tiles were first imported from the Low Countries in the 13th century, mainly in the east and south of the country until the late 1500s. By this time they had become standardized to approximately 10½ inches x 6½ inches. Increased imports, improved home production and the need for fire-proof coverings meant that they became more widespread during the 17th century, falling from favour due to competition from slates in the late 18th century. The revival of traditional materials in the late 19th century made them popular again until the 1950s.

Pantiles, with their distinctive wavy profile, became widespread down the east coast from the early 1600s, being especially popular in East Anglia, where glazed black versions were often fitted in the 18th century. By this time, home-produced types were available, and fixed at 13½ inches x 9½ inches by Act of Parliament; they became common in Yorkshire and Somerset.

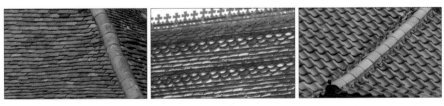

FIG 3.17: *Traditional hand-made clay tiles (left) have been used since the medieval period, but in the second half of the 19th century new machine-made types began taking over from slate, with patterned bands (centre) popular in the 1870s and 1880s. Pantiles with a wavy profile have been used in the eastern counties for centuries although most are more modern, green glazed machine-made types distinctive of the 1930s (right).*

CHAPTER 4
Windows, Doors and Decorative Details

The final pieces of the picture which make up the exterior of the house are the windows, doors and decorative elements. Their form and style have changed frequently throughout the centuries to suit fashion and regulations, and can be useful in helping to date a house. However, there is a problem with these fittings in that they are easy to change, just as relatively modern houses today can have replacement double glazing, upvc doors and stone cladding added, so owners in the past did the same to modernise or make the façade fashionable. Sometimes you can tell from clumsy proportions or misaligned windows that they were not part of the original design. Also, by looking at similar buildings in the area, you can often see an example which shows how they would have originally appeared. Dating these details is important because even if they do not tally with the original structure, they can help record a period of prosperity or a major rebuilding of the house which you may later be able to tie in with a change of owner or an improvement in the local area.

WINDOWS
The word 'window' is of Saxon origin and means 'wind eyes' or 'wind doors' which emphasises that the priority was for ventilation rather than as a source light. During

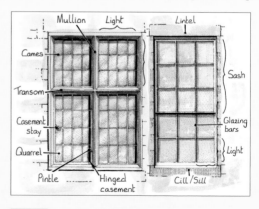

FIG 4.1: *Early windows were divided by vertical mullions and in the finest horizontal transoms as well, creating numerous openings called lights. In sash windows which dominate housing in the 18th and 19th centuries the two sashes were divided up by glazing bars to create individual lights.*

FIG 4.2: *A series of windows of diminishing width up the end gable of a house is characteristic of 17th-century houses.*

FIG 4.3: *Although some owners blocked up openings to reduce their Window tax contribution, many did this when also making internal changes like a new staircase (bricks will not line up, may be bigger and are flush with surrounding wall as in this example). Those which are recessed and line up with the course in the wall are usually part of the original design in order to maintain the symmetry while giving greater freedom for the internal layout.*

the medieval and Tudor period, with little attention paid to the proportions of the exterior, the size and position of windows reflected the importance of the room behind them: from tall imposing ones at the lord's end of the hall down to small insignificant openings in storage rooms. As the Classical orders and symmetry began to control the design of the façade from the 17th century, so windows were set in rigid positions and the rooms they illuminated and ventilated had to fit within these limitations. They also became subject to taxation from 1695 when excise duty on glass was introduced and the notorious Window Tax imposed on houses with a certain number of glazed openings (the threshold varied over the 150 years it was applied) and was finally abolished in 1851. Regulations and building acts to reduce fire risk also affected the setting of windows within the wall and this can be useful in dating houses. The end of taxation, relaxation of regulations, and cheaper glass resulted in a flourishing of different styles and sizes of windows from the second half of the 19th century.

Mullion Windows

A form of window popular during the medieval period, and which can still be found today, is a small opening divided up by vertical, square posts, set at 45° in the frame, called mullions. Although they might now have gone, the diamond-shaped socket in the sill can often be found. In the finest houses, decorative timber pieces were often inserted at the top to make each light appear like an arch. In areas with good stone, a separate frame and mullions were fitted within the wall but on timber-framed houses the top, bottom and sides were part of the structure, with just the mullion inserted (timber was used where the house was made of hard stones like granite). In early brick buildings the mullion could be made from the same material as the walls but might have been plastered over to make it look like stone. By the 16th century on the finest houses and by the 17th on most middling ones, real stone was used to make the frames.

As glass became common in higher status buildings during the Tudor period so the mullion was set square and usually carved with a simple moulding down its length: a quadrant with a small right-angled projection at either end (ovolo) was distinctive of the late 16th and early 17th centuries. Most ranged from two to five lights' width, one of these having a hinged frame for ventilation called a casement. In stone windows this would swing off a separate frame set in the opening but in timber it would be hung on iron pintles (a vertical pin on a horizontal bracket) directly fixed to the mullions; marks left by these might still be found today. These simple windows fell from favour in the 17th century and were relegated down the side or rear of houses but they continued to be used on rural cottages and farm buildings through into the early 19th century. Mullion windows were revived by Arts and Crafts

FIG 4.4: *From the 16th to the mid-17th century the mullions usually had mouldings down the side (top). Examples used on more humble buildings may survive from the 18th century when they tend to have a simple chamfer and in the 19th century when they are just square. Arts and Crafts architects reintroduced this form of window onto high class building but the mullions tend to have simple square profiles, a chamfer (bottom) or just a discreet moulding which is still sharp today. In the Cotswolds and the Pennines during the early 17th century the central mullion might be larger than the others, while from a little bit earlier, in Lancashire and Yorkshire, a round arch head was popular in each light through to the same period.*

architects from the 1870s up to the early 1900s with distinctive, long rows of sharp, square-edged (occasionally with discreet moulding) mullions, often with rectangular leaded lights and coloured glass patterns.

Some of the largest mullion windows, in the Pennines in particular, could have up to twenty lights and required an additional horizontal member called a transom. In the mid-17th century a new tall rectangular style of window appeared, with a single central mullion and transom. These cross windows became widespread by the 1690s

FIG 4.5: *Small oval windows were popular in the late 17th and early 18th centuries, especially in the 1690s.*

and were still being fitted well into the following century (see Fig 4.1, p56). The outer face of the cross could be chamfered or moulded but many were just squared off with a rebate on the inner edge to take the glazing. The transoms tend to be near to the centre on earlier examples but further towards the top on later types.

Sash Windows

A more graceful and practical solution appeared in the 1670s in the form of sash windows, at first only in a few select properties but quickly becoming more widespread by the early 18th century. The word 'sash' comes from the French word 'chassis' meaning a frame and the windows were made with two overlapping vertical frames divided up by glazing bars which held the individual panes of glass. In early types only the bottom one moved up and down but, by the mid-18th century, it was common for both to be moveable (double-hung). The size of glass, thickness of glazing bars and the setting of the sash box itself can help to date the windows and often the section of the house they are set in, but be warned, as it was common for the older cross windows which were of similar dimensions to be knocked out and replaced by sash windows at a later date.

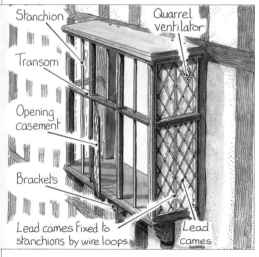

Stanchion

Transom

Opening casement

Brackets

Lead cames fixed to stanchions by wire loops

Quarrel ventilator

Lead cames

FIG 4.6: *Oriel windows which projected out from the wall (but did not rest upon the ground like a bay) and plant-on windows which did not stick out so much were the height of fashion on late medieval and Tudor houses and were still being fitted in the mid-17th century. They could be found on stone and brick buildings but were very popular on timber-framed houses. Although many have been replaced, the sockets for the brackets may survive in the timber frame below to reveal where they have been removed. Narrow flanking lights either side of oriels and other large windows were popular in the late 16th and early 17th centuries.*

The earliest sash windows had thick glazing bars up to 2 inches across with a simple moulding facing inwards (usually ovolo) and a tongue outwards onto which the glass was set with the putty chamfered up to hold it in place. The bars begin to get progressively thinner during the 18th century such that by the Regency period some are as little at ½ inch across (some had metal rods inserted for strength). The sash box was originally set so that its outer face was flush with the wall. However, with the 1709 London Building Act, they were set back 4 inches to reduce the risk of fire spreading across the façade and then, with the 1774 Building Act, the box itself had to be fitted behind the brickwork. These dates work well in London but were usually adopted by major towns and other cities in the following decades. In a few places it took even longer, while in the city of Bath the sashes had always been fitted behind the masonry. The number of individual panes or lights set within the sash also changed. Earlier types had between 9 and 16 small panes of glass in each sash (therefore 18 to 32 in total in a window), but by the Regency period 6 or 9 larger pieces in each is more common.

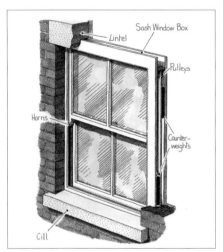

FIG 4.7: *A drawing of a Victorian sash, with labels of its parts. Some early sashes were just held in place by pegs but most were counterbalanced. If you get a chance to remove your sash windows for maintenance (getting them cleaned and fitted with inset insulation makes them comparable with double glazing for energy efficiency), then take a look at the workings down the side. The earliest examples had the groove for the cords carved out of a solid piece of wood, later ones had a box formed out of separate pieces, while the pulleys at the top were made of wood and weights from lead up until 1760s when cast-iron and brass begin to take over for both.*

Victorian sashes differed as glass became available in larger sizes and window taxes were abolished. During the 1850s, windows with just two panes in each sash became fashionable (see Fig 2.13, right) and, by the 1870s, ones with just a single sheet in each were common (Fig 2.23). Although these windows gave occupants an uninterrupted view, the fashionable Queen Anne style of the 1880s and '90s required glazing bars so architects came up with the compromise of leaving the lower pane clear and having just the upper sash divided up (Fig 2.27) – a very distinctive feature of the late Victorian and Edwardian periods.

Casements

Although sash windows were dominant during the 18th and 19th centuries, casement windows, fitted into one of the

FIG 4.8: *Examples of sash windows before the 1709 Building Act (left), before the 1774 Act (centre) and after it, when the box was set fully behind the brickwork (right). By the late 19th century relaxation in rules meant windows could once again be set flush or even project, imitating earlier styles.*

FIG 4.9: *Segmental arched tops were popular in the 1720s and '30s (left), round arched sash windows were common above staircases from the 1730s and along the façade in some late 18th- and early 19th-century houses (centre). Full height sashes which stretched down to the floor appeared in the 1770s and became common by the turn of the century (right).*

FIG 4.10: *From the mid-19th century the use of heavier, large pieces of glass without the stiffening effect from the glazing bars made the frame of the sash fragile. Therefore, the vertical side of the upper sash was extended a couple of inches down each side so the joint with the bottom bar could be strengthened. These protrusions were usually carved and are known as horns (left). Later, when windows with glazing bars once again became fashionable, carpenters still fitted horns so the presence of these can help identify later types of sash windows from pre-Victorian ones.*

FIG 4.11: *Venetian windows (left) with a central arch were especially popular in the late 18th century although they were also fitted prior to this date. A pair of narrow windows called margin lights either side of a main one became popular in the 1850s and 1860s and a similar effect was achieved by positioning two vertical glazing bars to the side of each sash creating narrow margins with coloured glass (centre); these Oxford windows being especially popular above staircases on late Victorian and Edwardian houses. Cheaper to make horizontal sliding sashes, known as Yorkshire sashes, were popular in late 18th- and early 19th-century rural and mill workers' cottages.*

FIG 4.12: *Casement windows often had segmental arches above on late 18th- and early 19th-century estate and urban cottages (left) and a wide pointed arch to suit the Gothick style usually with a distinctive Y-shaped glazing bar(centre left). A revival of Elizabethan and Gothic styles in the 1830s and 1840s made hood moulded types with shallow arches popular (centre) while by the mid-19th century, patterns formed by glazing bars were common on estate cottages (centre right). The fashion for casement windows from the 1890s coincided with the relaxing of rules on recessing windows and projecting frames which were fitted to many Edwardian houses (right).*

lights on mullion and cross windows, also became common. They were widely used for dormers, smaller properties especially cottages, upper stories on mill-workers houses and on larger properties in out-of-the-way places. A fixed wooden frame and glazing bars with one half hinged was a popular form from the end of the 17th century, with iron versions also produced in the late 18th and 19th centuries and

FIG 4.13: *Dormers became a fashionable feature of late 17th-century large houses and were widely used on later urban terraces to illuminate the attic and on 18th- and early 19th-century rural cottages. The top example is on a very steep pitched roof typical of the 1860s and 1870s; the bottom example is an eyebrow dormer popular at the turn of the 20th century.*

mainly fitted to rural cottages. As a traditional form of window they became popular again from the late 19th century, and replaced sash windows as the standard form on housing by the 1920s. These later types typically had a tall rectangular section with a small opening at the top which often featured coloured-glass patterns. In the 1930s and into the 1950s, steel frames with a strong horizontal emphasis were popular.

Glass

During the medieval period, shutters, animal skins or oiled fabric were used to close off windows from draughts, with glass being a luxury reserved for the church and the finest houses (the remains of grooves where internal shutters used to run can sometimes be found). Until an Act of 1579 made windows a permanent fixture, glass was of such value that when the gentry moved from one house to the other they would take their windows with them! The glass which was produced from the 13th century was generally poor compared with imports from Italy and the Low Countries and it was not until the Tudor period when immigrants from these countries established glassworks here that quality improved and glass became available to the merchant class. Although glass had become widely available by the 18th century, a levy from 1695 and excise duty from 1745 coupled with the Window Tax limited extravagant use until the mid-19th century when these restrictions were dropped at the same time as the mass production of larger sheets made it cheaper.

Early glass was made by hand, blowing down a tube to open up a ball of molten glass at the other end. With crown glass this was spun to form a disc which was cut into panes up to 10 inches across, with the central raised part (known as the crown, bullion or bull's-eye) thrown back in to be re-used. This part is now associated with imitation old windows but would rarely have been used in houses at the time. Another method was cylinder glass in which a long tube was formed

FIG 4.14: *Bay windows had featured on medieval halls and on large 16th- and early 17th-century houses but they grew in popularity from the late 18th century, some angled (left); others especially in the Regency period with a shallow bow (centre left). Victorian examples tend to be angled or squared, often with the windows above lining up with them (centre right). Bays with a deep semi circular plan were introduced in the Edwardian period and were very popular on inter-war semis (right), by which time they were fitted with casement windows rather than sashes.*

by swinging the molten glass through a pit whilst blowing and then cutting the ends off and opening out the cylinder to make a flat sheet. The glass produced in the 16th and 17th centuries tends to have a yellow or green tinge, fine air bubbles trapped within it and an uneven surface. It was typically cut into diamonds until rectangular panes became popular from the later 17th century. A better quality

FIG 4.15: *You can usually tell old from new glass simply by letting it catch the light and comparing the flat smooth surface of modern float glass with the slightly rippled or undulating surface of glass produced in previous centuries. The oldest glass as in this example from the early 17th century has the distinctive green tinge, fine air bubbles and ripples indicating it was made from a spun disc; larger Victorian pieces are clearer but can still have a slightly undulating surface.*

glass could be produced by polishing and grinding a large piece, this plate glass remaining a luxury product until improved manufacturing techniques in the Victorian period.

Fittings and Surrounds

Before glazing bars became widely used in the early 18th century, the small panes of glass (quarrels) were held in place by thin strips of lead (cames). As this lattice was rather fragile, a vertical wood or iron rod (a stanchion) was usually placed in front of the centre of a light with small pieces of wire attaching it to the lead. The socket for these can often still be found in the frame above or below a mullion window (medieval windows sometimes had metal security grills and the marks left by these can also be found). Later windows might have had a saddle bar fitted horizontally across with its flattened end nailed to the wooden frame.

One problem with windows was keeping rainwater running down the face of a wall from flowing into the window. On Tudor and Stuart houses a hood mould was usually fitted, a horizontal moulding with L-shaped ends above each opening (see Fig 2.17 left). However, by the late 17th century, it became fashionable for one long string course (a projecting horizontal band) to be fitted above them (see Fig 2.17 top right). During the early Georgian and early Victorian periods there were various mouldings and pediments which could be applied around window openings in the finest classical houses (see Fig 2.25), while bay windows in the second half of the

FIG 4.16: *In the late Victorian period it became fashionable to insert coloured glass patterns into the upper section of casement windows and glazed front doors. Art Nouveau flowing floral patterns (top) and heraldic symbols were popular initially; by the 1930s more geometric and Art Deco designs were common (bottom). As with all houses, windows could be updated at any time and it is common to find these patterned windows on earlier properties.*

FIG 4.17: *In early houses, shutters were fitted on the inside (left) and remains of the rebates or peg holes where the timber grooves were once fitted can sometimes be found. Original external shutters seem to date from the 18th and early 19th centuries and the iron stays (centre left) which held them back and the pintles on which they were hung (centre right) often survive on the outside. Blinds were often fitted on the outside of Regency and early Victorian houses to shade the inside from the sun, the boxes in which they were held often survive on top of sash windows (right).*

19th century could be flanked by columns with capitals reflecting the style of house (see Fig 2.23).

DOORS

Doors are another datable feature of a house although, more than any other feature, they are liable to be replaced due to wear or fashion; some, which might look genuine, may have been picked up from a reclamation yard and fitted in more recent years. It is also important to look for old doorways which have been blocked up as the internal arrangement has altered. The door surround is more likely to be original and in timber-framed houses the side pieces (the jambs) and the door head above were part of the structure of the wall with the door larger than the opening and resting up against its inside face when closed.

Doorways in a large Tudor house may have had the edges to the jambs moulded (ovolo was popular from the mid 16th century) with this detail ending just short of the floor in a decorative terminal known as a stop. (These are datable: see Linda Hall's book *Period House Fixtures and Fittings*.) The door head was often carved with an arch, noticeably pointed in the late medieval period, flatter with barely a curve in the 16th and early 17th centuries (a date might also be carved on this feature). Similar designs were used in stone doorways of the same period although

FIG 4.18: *The style of doorhead changed over the centuries and varied in the regions. Four centred arches were noticeably curved in the 15th century (left) but became very flat during the 16th century. Ogee doorheads (centre) were common in the west and north in the late 15th and 16th centuries. Cambered heads (right) date from the mid-16th to mid-17th centuries before square headed doorways, which had always been used for lesser entrances, begin to dominate all openings during the 17th century.*

round arches could be found on the grandest classical houses. Square-headed doorways began to replace those with a shallow arch elsewhere from around this time. In the late 17th century, door cases became fashionable, with moulded pieces of timber placed around the inside edge and faces of an opening through a brick, stone or stud wall (as they still are in modern houses), with the door now recessed within the opening (Fig 4.19).

The door itself in medieval and Tudor houses was typically made from vertical planks held in place by battens across the inside face although better-quality doors may have been double thickness, with horizontal planks covering the inside rather than just battens.The earliest tend to have just two or three vertical planks of irregular width, four or five were common by the late 17th century and then six or more in the 19th century when they were regular machine-cut pieces. These were butted up against each other with, on the finest doors, thin wooden fillets fixed on

FIG 4.19: *The earliest doorcases had bolection moulding (left) typical of the period 1670 to 1720, Gibbs surrounds were popular in the mid-18th century (centre) and reeded doorcases with bulls eyes in the corners (right) are distinctive of the Regency period. Early external ones were made from wood but Building Acts meant they were made from stone or plaster after 1709.*

top of the gaps to cover them up. Later in the 18th and 19th centuries, a beading was cut along one edge covering the joint between the two. The heads of the nails which held them together were sometimes arranged in patterns. Later plank and batten doors, however, were only used on cheaper properties or for the service areas of larger ones.

By the late 17th century, panelled doors with a framework and panels fitted within it began to be found in the most fashionable houses (often quite squat looking as in Fig 4.19 left), although some plank and batten doors already had strips nailed across the front to imitate this type of door. By the 18th century, panelled doors were standard in all but the cheapest houses, with six panels distinctive of the Georgian period, four, six or even eight in the Regency but four becoming dominant by the Victorian. The wide variety of styles during the 19th century often meant that the door was adapted to suit: plank and batten doors could be found on Gothic and Arts and Crafts houses but with straight machine cuts and regular width they clearly differ from earlier types while the six-panelled door reappears on the Neo-Georgian houses of the early 20th century.

Since doors are very easy to replace, they should be used with caution for dating purposes. However, looking at neighbouring properties for identical types can often establish if it is an original fitting (or if the entire row was renovated at the same time, the style of the door may help date the renovation). In general the front door

FIG 4.20: *Examples of some of the more common types of door:16th-century plank and batten (left) with distinctive wide planks, a six-panelled Georgian door (centre left), a four-panelled mid Victorian door (centre), a glazed Edwardian door (centre right) and a 1930s' door with the tall panels at the bottom and glazed upper third (right). Some rural properties can be found with extra wide doors which might indicate that this was for access to a byre or barn to let cattle through. Also, look for the outer frame to be of unequal widths or for the panels not being symmetrical which indicates that the door has been cut down to fit the opening and is not in its original location.*

and those into main reception rooms would have had the finest detail, with the edges to the panels moulded. The face into a service room or lesser bedroom would usually not have these details so if you find one like this in a prominent position there is a good chance it has been moved.

Porches and Hoods

Building a porch in front of the doorway was more than a way of reducing draughts, it was a grand

FIG 4.21: *A late 17th-century hood (top left), a Regency iron porch (above) and an Edwardian type (left), with distinctive white timber fretwork.*

entrance designed to impress. Medieval halls had them added at the lower end (with the façade often balanced with a tall window or bay at the high end, see Fig 2.15). Large Tudor and Stuart houses had a tall central one, with fashionable classical details like columns crudely stacked up on top of each other. In the late 17th and early 18th centuries large semi-circular hoods with shell-like undersides and large ornate brackets were very distinctive. Georgian façades were often plain, with some later ones having a pedimented porch, and intricate iron types in the Regency period. An open flat-roofed porch supported on columns and pilasters (flat columns built into the wall) imitating a classical portico were popular on large terraced houses in the first half of the 19th century (see Fig 2.25). A variety of hoods was added to Victorian Gothic houses, some with steep-pitched tiled roofs and others appearing like beaten metal helmets. In the late 19th century, the door began to be recessed back so that a short porch was formed within the body of the house with the flanks often covered with decorative tiles (see Fig 2.23). Those with a wide-arched opening are distinctive of Arts and Crafts houses; white-painted timber hoods and porches were common on Edwardian properties; and semi-circular arched porches were popular on 1930s' semis.

Door Furniture

Long strap hinges were a key part of plank and batten doors, with one end bent around to fit over the iron pintle in the doorframe. The form and decoration of the hinge changed through the centuries. For instance, a diamond- or lozenge-shaped end was popular from the late 16th century for a hundred years or so and decorative details were cut or stamped in them during the mid-17th century. Later ones tend to have a more pronounced taper to them and are plain. By the 19th century, they have a steeply-angled top and bottom edge and are machine-made.

Most door knockers and handles will have been replaced on old properties although the marks, holes or old metal back plates might survive to show where fittings have previously been. Security has always been a problem for those with items worth stealing, and door locks or the holes where they were once fitted can sometimes be found. Cash was often kept in farmhouses (they loaned money to neighbours in the days before banks became widespread) so sockets in the doorframe can reveal where a drawbar was once fitted to the back of the door. Letter boxes were introduced from the 1840s: early ones were often small and they did not become standard until the end of the century. Some that seem clumsily fitted or squeezed in may indicate that they were fitted into an existing door.

Fanlights

As double piled houses became popular in the late 17th century, the hallway became darker as rear windows were further back. To counter this, a small window was fitted above the front door (or, in some older properties where space was limited, the door was cut down in height to accommodate the window) and were simple

FIG 4.22: *A distinctive feature of late Georgian and Regency terraces is ironwork around the entrance. A narrow cone on a bracket (link snuffers) used by link boys to put out the torches with which they guided the wealthy home were popular from the 1770s (left); arches with a circular bracket used to hold lanterns were also common (right) and boot scrapers were a standard fitment on most houses into the late Victorian period as the roads were filthy and pavements not always provided.*

FIG 4.23: *Iron railings helped stop people falling down the void in front of the basement (the area) and became a decorative feature even on later houses without one. The railings were collected for scrap metal in the Second World War, so many today are later replacements. Original ones usually only had a single horizontal bar at the top; later replacements usually have them top and bottom.*

FIG 4.24: *A late 17th-century overlight (top), a mid-18th-century fanlight (centre) and a late Georgian type with intricate casting (bottom).*

rectangular openings with a mullion and leaded lights. By the early 18th century, they were fitted with glazing bars mirroring the fashion in windows. If the moulding on these still matches the windows, then it can indicate that they are all original as these over lights were rarely changed. From the 1760s, semicircular types began to appear, divided up by radiating glazing bars which made them look like a fan, (hence the word 'fanlight', although this term is often used for all types of over lights), with ever more intricate patterns appearing as wood was replaced by wrought iron and brass. Mass produced cast-iron pieces were introduced from the late 18th century and the simple fanlight could be found on cheaper properties into the early Victorian period. By this time, fashionable classical houses now had porticos in front of the door so the plain rectangular over light was fitted, becoming popular on mid-Victorian houses, often with the house number or name on the glass (house numbering was introduced in London during the 18th century but only became widespread elsewhere in the 19th). Glazed doors in the late Victorian period meant over lights were unnecessary although they were still fitted to many Edwardian houses, not dying out completely until the 1930s.

Chimneys

As the fireplace and chimney stack were such a major and integral part of most old houses they were rarely rebuilt and their position, construction and style can be a vital clue to the original form and date of a building. In this chapter we are interested in the visible top section which protrudes above the roof – the chimney – and it is this part being more vulnerable to the elements which could have been replaced or shortened due to damage, had chimney pots added, or been rebuilt when the house had a major make-over. However, in most cases, the base of it at least will be contemporary with the original building.

In the Tudor period they were a status symbol and owners had distinctive tall stacks with cylindrical and polygonal stone or decorated brick chimneys high above the roof line of the finest houses. The new houses of the merchant and yeoman farmer class during the late 16th and 17th centuries would often imitate these but on a smaller scale. They were usually without the expensive decoration, though, like their larger counterparts, the chimneys would rise from a square base with an individual one for each fireplace. As they became widespread and the Classical styles began to dominate from the early 18th century, the chimney was no longer regarded as a feature for display and shorter, plain rectangular stacks containing a number of separate flues was common in the Georgian and into the Victorian period. They were built within the walls either at the end gables or in the walls which divided the front from the back room and were hidden from view behind the parapet.

Fashionable Regency villas often had hipped roofs which meant the stack was rather prominent at the sides as the top of a chimney should be above the ridge of the roof in order to get a good draw (although this has not always been appreciated in the past). Lightweight pots may have first been added here in order to extend the height, a fashion which became widespread in the 19th century, with a variety of types

FIG 4.25: *A 17th-century axial stack (left) with its distinctive stocky base and individual chimneys on top. Georgian and Regency ones (centre left) tend to be plain (although Gothick types mirrored Tudor styles) but the Victorians made a feature of them once Classical parapets fell from favour with pots (centre right) now added to improve draw (debatable to what extent they did) and, in the late 19th century, huge stacks were a key part of the design of the house (right). Late Victorian and Edwardian houses had the stacks positioned so they came straight up halfway down the slope of the roof.*

FIG 4.26: *Bargeboards were fitted to protect the vulnerable edge of a gabled roof and they were very popular in Victorian times, often being added to older properties. Look for sharper edged wood compared with the rest of the house (bottom left). Early Victorian types tend to be deeply carved (top left), later ones are more subtle (top right) and Edwardian ones plainer still.*

claiming to improve the performance of the fire below, especially now that coal which requires extra combustion was in widespread use. Victorian builders had a better understanding of chimney stack design and made the flue narrower and avoided unnecessary twists and turns. Now that the parapet had fallen from favour, chimneys once again became a prominent feature, decorated to suit the style of house and reaching a zenith in size during the late 19th century where they could dwarf the house below. By the 1930s, as electric, gas and portable paraffin heaters became available, the chimney once again was relegated in importance and there tends to be one simple central stack and a tall thin one towards the rear corner to serve the kitchen range or hot water boiler (this is often gone today as they were precarious on a hipped roof). Although fewer chimneys were fitted after the 1960s when central heating became common, they have once again risen in popularity as our primeval love of the fire as a key element of the interior has made a single stack a fashionable addition.

Decorative Elements

There are numerous additions made to the façade of a house over the centuries which can help date that part of the house. Some were regional styles which do not necessarily sit in one particular period but many were fashionable decorative elements which can be more accurately pinpointed. The following illustrations are just some of the most common.

FIG 4.28: *Decorative plaques and bands have often been added to houses to enliven the façade. In the late 18th century Adams-style roundels and Neo Georgian designs (top) were popular; in the mid-19th century it was Gothic motifs (centre) while during the late Victorian period terracotta bands (bottom) and plaques were commonly applied.*

FIG 4.27: *Turrets were distinctive features of late Victorian houses. They were mostly square or cylindrical, with steep conical caps imitating those fitted to Scottish baronial-style buildings (this style was popular at the time on commercial and public buildings but less often on domestic properties).*

FIG 4.29: *The rainwater trap at the top of the vertical gutter pipe was a prominent feature on the front of early 18th-century houses (left). The idea was revived by Arts and Crafts architects in the late 19th century with distinctive foliage patterns.*

FIG 4.30: *Balconies were fashionable in the late 18th and early 19th centuries when occupants wanted to observe passers-by and take in the air, especially in trendy city squares and seaside resorts. Some were built with stone or stucco-covered balustrades while in the Regency period iron railings were popular (top). However, as the Victorians sought privacy so they fell from favour only becoming fashionable again on the more lively Edwardian façades, usually with white-painted wooden railings (left).*

CHAPTER 5
The Interior and Fittings

The interior will usually have fewer clues by which to date the house than the exterior simply because it is more prone to a 'make-over'. The wide range of shops and books encouraging you to transform the inside of your home is nothing new; people have always updated or enlarged the interiors of their houses to suit changing fashions in decoration and arrangements of rooms. It was also common in the past for houses which had fallen from fashion or were in areas which had dropped in popularity to be split up into cheap accommodation; these transitions causing much destruction of original fittings and forms. Some have remained thus, while others have been returned to their original glory in more recent times.

A few can be found reasonably untouched by later work, but most will have been redecorated a number of times. However, you might often find original fittings such as doors, stairs, and wall mouldings (skirting boards, cornices and rails) which can help to date that part of the house or at least a time when there was a major renovation. It also pays to make a note of the quality of the fittings: people will

FIG 5.1: *A late Victorian interior, with labels of the key features which can be found in period houses.*

always put their best face on the public front, so the hallway and principal reception rooms would have the finest fireplace, doors and wall mouldings, whereas those in the service rooms and minor bedrooms would be plain.

A BRIEF HISTORY

The story of the inside of houses since the Tudor period up to the 1930s is of a shift from communal living to one of greater privacy, with separate rooms rather than an open plan. The interior of most medieval houses was based around one principal room – the hall – a rectangular open space in which the household – comprising the family, its entourage and servants – ate, talked and slept together, with the main difference between those of the local gentry and the poor farmers being size. The wealthy would have private chambers off the hall but these took time to work their way down the social ladder, with many of the working classes still renting a single room for the whole family into the early 19th century. While the Stuart gentry built themselves suites of rooms to entertain guests, the new homes of merchants and yeoman farmers would be more modest, with two or three downstairs rooms, one in which the cooking and eating took place and another for conversation – the parlour, a smart room which was still desired by the working classes well into the 20th century.

FIG 5.2: *Look for signs of changes to rooms where old walls have been knocked through (as in this case where an extension has been added and the old vertical timbers cut through to form a doorway into it). Internal walls could also be inserted into a ground floor room, perhaps to create a lobby or divide a large room. Where the fireplace is off centre or close to a wall junction this might indicate where this has happened. Also look at ceiling beams; if the moulding goes through then it could be a later wall; if they stop short of it then it should be original.*

By the 18th century a clear division between the family and servants could be seen in the houses of the better-off, with large urban terraces and rural detached homes having smart reception rooms to the front or on the first floor (piano nobile) while the service rooms were out of the way in the basement or rear of the building. There was a distinctive masculine and feminine split, with the dining room usually decorated with rich furnishings and stronger colour schemes, while the drawing room to which the ladies withdrew after a meal had a more delicate and lighter feel. The idea of going up to bed only became common in this period as separate bedrooms above parlours and living rooms were fitted in all but the poorest housing. By the Regency period greater privacy for the family was usually achieved by providing

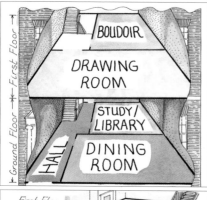

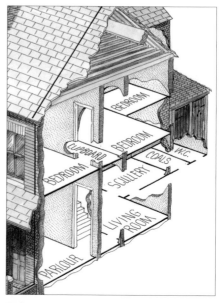

FIG 5.4: *A cut-away view of a late Victorian terrace. This is a big step up for a working class family from the single rooms many families in this class lived in earlier in the 19th century. It has a separate scullery for washing and laundry, a living room with a small range cooker and a parlour reserved for the best furniture and special occasions. There was no bathroom, although one was often added later in the bedroom above the scullery.*

FIG 5.3: *A cut-away view of a Georgian terrace interior (top) and a Regency one (bottom). The reception rooms in larger houses were usually on the first floor, the piano nobile, as the hall made the ground floor rooms smaller.*

a separate staircase at the rear so that servants could come and go without getting in the way of the family or guests.

During the 19th century an increasing number of rooms with a specific use appeared at the top end of the market. A morning or breakfast room, a library and a study were common, and compact versions of these were sometimes squeezed into more modest middle class homes. Changes also came about thanks to widespread improvements in water supply and sewerage: the kitchen and scullery could now be brought out of the basement and fitted into rear extensions. By the Edwardian period they were being positioned within the house itself (it was common for the

FIG 5.5: *Toilets were little more than a hole above a cesspit in the yard or a bucket (as in this Victorian example) emptied into a convenient dung heap in most houses before the late 19th century. Inside a chamber pot (or a commode for the better off) was used at night time. A water closet (W.C.) only became widespread in the late Victorian period when sewerage and a more powerful water supply meant it could be fitted upstairs in middle class houses, and from the 1920s in new working class housing.*

door into the service area to be plain on one side and moulded or fielded on the side facing guests). Bathrooms became common in late Victorian middle class homes but they did not become a standard fitting in the homes of the poor until after the Second World War. Alongside the bathroom was a separate room where flushing water closets were fitted.

A key change during the 20th century was architects trying to force open-plan living on an unwilling public. New houses and flats for the working classes were laid out with one large living space (which was a better use of the limited room available) but it has only been since the widespread adoption of central heating from the 1960s that the idea has proved popular.

INTERIOR STRUCTURES AND FITTINGS
Walls
The interior surface of the walls of timber-framed houses would usually have been lime- or colour-washed, sometimes with text or pictures painted directly upon it. In the finest rooms wooden panelling was used to help insulate and add a touch of

FIG 5.6: *Despite the demise of timber framing, most non load bearing internal walls in 18th- and 19th-century houses (and some load bearing ones too) were made from a timber framework covered with thin strips of wood called laths which acted as a key for the finished plaster surface. Earlier laths were hand cut and rough edged (left), 19th-century ones were machine cut and straighter (right). By the 1920s blocks made from breeze or cinders were a quick and cheap alternative and in modern houses concrete blocks are also used for load bearing walls.*

FIG 5.7: *Linenfold and plain square panelling (left) with a moulding around the top and sides and a flat chamfer at the bottom (to make it easier to dust) was common in the finest 16th-century houses. (When old panelling has been put into another house it is common to find the plain chamfer is not on the bottom indicating it has been moved from somewhere else.). Fielded panels (centre) become more common in the early 17th century, the decorative pattern down the left side of this example is strapwork which is distinctive of late 16th- and early 17th-century houses (and some Tudor style ones from the 1830s and 1840s). Classical proportions (right) became popular in the late 17th and early 18th centuries. Skirting boards were never fitted on original panelling; if found they will be later additions or can indicate replica work.*

class. Small square panels appear in the mid-15th century set in a framework and held together by two pegs on each joint (modern replicas often only have one). By the late 17th century, the proportions of the panelling changed to suit classical styles, with tall central panels above a dado rail. From around 1700 these were made from pine, and painted or stained a dark colour (original softwood panelling or fittings were never left with their grain and knots exposed). Panelling fell from favour during the 18th century as wallpapers, paint and fabric coverings became available. However, it was still used in many houses underneath the dado rail to protect the wall from the backs of chairs. In poorer housing vertical planks, usually with a single beading down one edge, were used from the late 18th century to line walls, either full height or just up to the chair rail.

Wallpaper was first developed in the 16th century as a cheaper alternative to tapestries for the finest houses. It became more popular amongst the middle classes in the 18th century, although it was still a luxury product being hand-printed on single strips of paper. Mass production and the introduction of continuous rolls made it affordable for many of the working classes later in the 19th century. A fragment of wallpaper discovered as the base layer under numerous later ones can be useful to help date that wall; try using catalogues online or sources like the Victoria and Albert Museum.

Walls have traditionally been divided up into sections by wooden and plaster mouldings for both decorative and protective measures. The dado or chair rail was fitted at a time when chairs were positioned around the edge of a room. By the 19th century, as they tended to be left around the table which was now a permanent feature in the centre of the room, it fell from use although it was still common in halls. The picture rail was used to hang paintings from and was popular in houses up to the Second World War. In the late 19th century and early 20th century it was distinctly lined up with the top of the door frame. Skirting boards were again introduced to protect the base of walls when new plastered and papered walls replaced panelling. Their profile and size varies through the ages and, where they appear original, can be roughly dated. Cornicing covered the joint between the ceiling and the wall (which could open up) and, as with other mouldings, the more ornate it is the more important the room.

Floors

The floor in most ordinary houses, even up to the middle of the 19th century, was often no more than beaten earth. The ground surface was mixed with lime, sand, clay or even bulls' blood. It was then raked over and drenched in water, before being left for a few weeks and finally beaten flat by paddles. Rushes or straw could be strewn over it to keep dust down and collect dirt. Don't be surprised to find these almost concrete-like floors under layers of later vinyls and ceramic tiles! In the finest medieval houses, red clay tiles around 6 inches square could be fitted and, from the Tudor period, brick was used to make some floors. Although these will be rare today their age can be determined by the size of the bricks and their general wear and tear. Flagstones were also reserved for the better-quality home but became more widely available from the late 17th century, working their way down the social scale over the next 200 years.

As many Georgian and Regency houses were raised above an underground room

FIG 5.8: *Encaustic (with a pattern formed by stamping it in wet clay and filling with a different colour clay) and geometric tiles were distinctive of Victorian halls and some reception rooms (blues and greens were absent from early examples). Black and white tiling was popular from the 1890s into the 1930s.*

FIG 5.9: *Parquet flooring has been used for centuries but was particularly popular in the late 19th and early 20th centuries.*

the family and reception rooms could have floorboards or stone slabs, with stone or brick in the basement. Machine-made ceramic tiles were the hallmark of Victorian houses, with companies like Mintons making hardwearing plain, multi-coloured and patterned tiles which were characteristic of hallways and some reception rooms. In the late Victorian period, as basements fell from favour and the floor was raised a foot or so above the ground to reduce damp (see Fig 3.1), floorboards were widely used, until in the first half of the 20th century as damp courses improved, concrete floors become common.

The upper floor in medieval houses was supported upon thick joists which were usually placed so that their wider side (which could be up to 8 inches) was facing upwards, a weaker arrangement but used to reduce the effect that the warping of the oak would have upon the floorboards fitted across it. After the mid-17th century they were fitted in the conventional manner with the thinner side facing upwards. Tudor joists tend to become thinner and more square in profile and, by the early 18th century, softwood takes over from oak, with most between 4–6 inches high and around 2 inches thick. By this time, as a fire precaution, it became good practice for joists to run from front to back rather than have their ends set into the party wall (which made it easier for fire to spread along a row of houses).

Floorboards have become narrower through the centuries; the earliest were around a foot across and could vary in width. Thinner tongued and grooved, machine-cut types have only been widespread in the past 100 years. In the finest rooms, the nails would be carefully positioned in the ends so they could not be seen when the next one was fitted, this was important since fully fitted carpets became common only from the 1960s; previously the floorboards would have been partly exposed around carpet pieces and rugs. If a good quality hardwood could not be used, then softwood planks were stained or painted to appear like hardwoods.

Ceilings
The height of rooms has varied through the ages. It has always been low or only as high as necessary in cheaper housing, but in the main reception rooms of finer Georgian and Victorian houses it was often as high as 10 feet or more until cost-cutting after the Second World War made lower ones standard. The ceiling in timber-framed houses was in fact the exposed undersides of the joists and

FIG 5.10: *The summer (from Saxon 'somer' which was derived from Latin for pack horse) or bridging beam was the main timber across the length of the house. It was usually left exposed with edges chamfered (left) or moulded (right). If ceiling timbers have sharp squared edges, they tend to be replicas or ones which were originally hidden underneath a plaster covering (the notches in the right example show it has once been plastered).*

floorboards of the storey above. In finer houses the beams could have been moulded with decorative bosses covering the junctions, while in some, panels were applied over the joists. In general, if you find beams or joists with a moulding or chamfer behind a ceiling, then these timbers were originally on show and the plaster covering is almost certainly of a later date. Plaster ceilings formed on laths applied to the underside of the joists began to be fitted in the finest houses from the 16th century but did not become universal until the 18th, only being finally replaced after the Second World War by plasterboard.

FIG 5.11: *Ceiling roses were used to cover up the marks left by gas and oil lamps upon the ceiling and, as a decorative feature, becoming especially popular in the Victorian period. Some were hollow and linked into vents in the floorboards so the fumes could be carried away. They become rare after the 1920s as electric lighting and lower ceilings became common.*

Fireplaces

In some of the finer medieval houses, smoke hoods were fitted which were basically a timber-framed funnel which directed the fumes up through the roof or a smoke bay in which one end of the room was screened off above head height trapping the fumes. If they survived, then it was common for the new fireplaces and flues to have been built within one of these earlier hoods or bays, or sometimes even in the screens passage which ran between the front and rear door.

Tudor and Stuart fireplaces have wide openings, sometimes large enough for seating (inglenooks) and often have a bread oven to the side (usually from the

FIG 5.12: *The fireplace or more precisely its surround is often changed to suit fashions and reclaimed ones fitted to blend in with the age of the property. Caution has to be taken when dating a room from the style of the fireplace. Its position and the size of the opening may be of greater help. Popular styles include four centred arches in the 16th and early 17th centuries (see FIG 5.14.a.), bolection moulding from the 1670s to the 1720s (top left), Adams styles with central plaques and classical details (top centre) in the late 18th century , and Regency types with bulls eyes in the corners (top right). Victorian fireplaces could be purchased in a wide range of styles, mid-19th century (bottom left) and Edwardian (bottom right). Note the mantel which is deep enough for ornaments and was a feature of Victorian surrounds but could be added to earlier ones.*

late 17th century). They either have shallow arches especially in the south and east, a large timber lintel (initials of married couples often carved on this), or a stone or brick surround. The wood being burned was held in fire dogs often with a cast-iron fire back to protect the stone or brickwork behind it.

From the 18th century coal became more widely available and it could be burnt in a smaller mass so compact metal grates were fitted. Later, registers were added with a flap above at the base of the flue which could control the draw. Although boys were sent up chimneys to clean them well into the 19th century, most flues on new houses were becoming narrower and carefully designed so as to improve the performance of the fire.

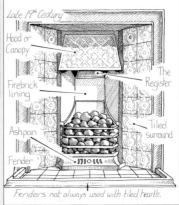

FIG 5.13: A Regency hob grate (left), a round arched grate from the mid-19th century (centre) and a late Victorian register grate with labels of parts (right). Firebrick linings (slow combustion grates) appeared from the 1850s, and an adjustable front canopy from the 1880s.

FIG 5.14: Overmantels above the fireplace were common in the finest houses in the late 16th (left) and 17th centuries (often incorporating distinctive Jacobean round arched patterns from 1610–40). They became popular once again in Edwardian houses inspired by Arts and Crafts architects (right).

Stairs

The most basic type of stairs which could be found in some medieval houses was little more than a ladder, with crude horizontal treads fixed between diagonal bearers. Only in the finest houses would stone spiral staircases be found. As an upstairs began to be incorporated into houses during the 16th and 17th centuries, so a wider range of solutions for ascending were devised. In large houses a projecting stair turret or porch could feature a closed well staircase, with flights of stairs wrapped around an enclosed central void (popular in lesser houses in the south from 1600–1650 and in the north some 50 years later). From the mid-17th century, as the stairs became a key feature on show at the back of the hall, these were opened up, with carved balusters, newel posts and plastered undersides making them a spectacular feature. More compact versions could be found in modest houses of the period. Winder stairs built into the tight space to the side of

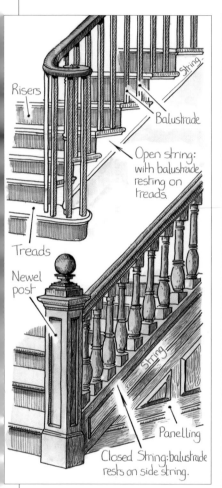

FIG 5.16: *The first turned balusters appeared in the late 16th century and they tend to be thick, with slender rings, and the top half mirroring the bottom until the mid-17th century when vase shapes became popular. Simpler versions could be carved out of a block or even just a plank known as splat balusters (left), most dating from the 17th century (those having pierced patterns tend to be late 17th century). Twisted balusters were popular from the 1670s to 1740s (centre left). Eighteenth-century turned balusters are more slender with vase shapes (centre right) and columns often with a urn form at the base and longer square unturned sections at top and bottom than earlier ones. Thin iron or wood balusters with a square section (right) were common in the late 18th and early 19th centuries.*

FIG 5.15: *A drawing of an open string (top) and closed string (bottom). The light and airy top example is distinctive of the Regency period while the heavier bottom example was common in the finest 17th-century houses and was widely imitated in the Victorian period (often in exotic woods like mahogany rather than oak).*

the fireplace with the treads fixed into the doorframe at the bottom were common and could still be found in small cottages in the 19th century. (Some of these have since been converted into a cupboard where a straight set has been added at a later date.)

Most of these 16th- and 17th-century staircases had closed strings, i.e. the balusters

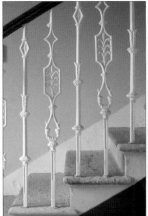

FIG 5.17: *Nineteenth-century balusters could be found in a wide range of historic styles. Regency cast-iron patterns (left), heavy wooden Victorian closed string stairs (centre) which tend to have thinner balusters than the originals, and Edwardian Arts and Crafts (right) with simplified designs were just some of the more common types.*

rested upon the bearers up the side into which the treads were fixed. From the early 18th century, however, more elegant open string stairs with the balusters resting on top of the tread became popular. Later Georgian and Regency types often have a distinctive widened bottom step, with a curved end and thin iron balusters with a dark wood handrail terminating in a spiral above it; and some have a glass lantern in the roof above to cast light down into the stairwell. Victorian staircases can be found in a wide range of styles as they revived closed string staircases and newel posts and, without an expert eye, it is often only through wear and tear or by identifying the type of wood (usually oak in the 17th century, pine in the 18th, and mahogany, teak and walnut in the 19th) that these replicas can be told apart from the earlier types. In most terraces the stairs were at the side or rear, trapped between rooms so there was little more than a handrail, but in the wider plot of the inter-war semi they were brought forward and made a feature of in the hall, with a simple painted balustrade down one side.

Lofts

These can be the most important room to investigate in an old house. The exposed timbers within can reveal much about how the house has developed and it has often been left untouched during later renovations. It might contain many original parts, the form of which can indicate the age of the property. Samples from the timbers can be analysed to give an accurate date (see dendrochronology, Chapter 7).

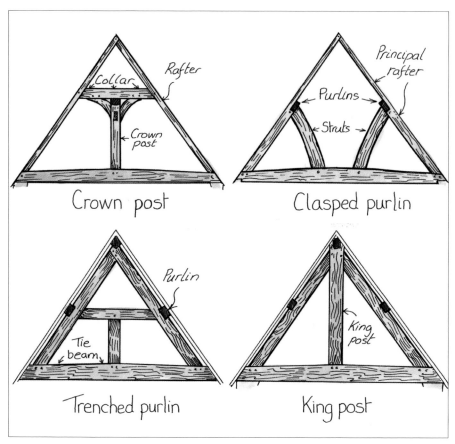

FIG 5.18: *The rafters, purlins, struts and tie beam can form a rigid structure called a truss which can be laid out in a line above the walls or can form part of a continuous roof structure as was common on terraces. Their arrangement changed over the centuries and although there are many regional variations, especially on earlier timber-framed buildings, there are some common types which are shown here. Along with condition and how regular the timbers are cut, they can help indicate which period they come from (the red highlighted parts are longitudinal timbers running along the length of the roof). Crown post roofs were popular in the south and east up to the early 16th century. Clasped purlin roofs superseded them in these areas, while in the west and parts of the north, trenched purlins took over from crucks frames at around the same time. King posts were popular in large buildings in the north from the medieval period onwards; they also became popular across the country in the 19th century. These will usually have smooth machine-cut timbers and iron bolts holding them together (see Fig 5.19).*

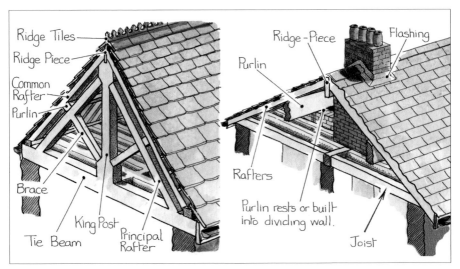

FIG 5.19: *Examples of the roof structure in Victorian terraces. Some larger houses with steep pitched roofs used king post trusses (left) while most common terraces had substantial purlins which rested upon or were built within the dividing walls to support the rafters and roof covering (right).*

When roofs are repaired or new coverings applied, rotten timbers will usually be replaced and, where this has been done in recent times, it should be clear by their condition or by their squared machine-cut form compared with pre-19th-century ones which are usually rougher in finish. Before the 1970s rafters, purlins, struts and tie beams were normally cut and assembled on site but, since then, prefabricated trusses have been brought complete to site with galvanised metal plates over the joints and these could have been used on an extension to an older building. Make note of other details like paint, old chimney breasts or partitions in the loft which could indicate where it might have been used for storage or as a bedroom in the past, or it might show where fireplaces were once sited below. It is also worth taking photos of the loft so that you can show a local expert in the field who may be able to shed more light on it.

SECTION II

SEARCHES

CHAPTER 6
The Basic Search:
Local Sources

The architectural details covered in the previous chapters can help you achieve a better understanding of how your house developed and in what period it was probably constructed. Documentation held in local, county and national archives, however, will usually be required to pinpoint the date further. This seemingly onerous task has been made easier in the past decade with the explosion of information on the Internet, as well as a wealth of publications with an increased interest in tracing family histories. As ever, the assistance available in the records offices themselves is always of value to the beginner. Before going online or driving off to one of these archives, it is well worth exhausting your local studies centre which is usually in the library (major cities may have separate record offices and the librarian will be able to advise you; or you can visit the library service on the local county council's website). This chapter outlines the first steps that you should make in researching the history of a house and lists some of the most common sources which are available locally.

Before starting, make a plan of the house and the plot within which it sits along the lines suggested in the preface of this book. Take lots of photos of the inside and outside, with close-ups of any details you think may be important or of interest, working from the overall history of the area down to the specific records of the house. If your house was part of a large estate, then you may find the records to this are held in the county which was home to the landowner and not where the building is physically located. (You may be able to get books or copies of documents from another

Notes when using archives

There are a few important points you should be aware of before going to your local studies centre or other archives:

* Always use a pencil when making notes, this is to stop getting any ink on your fingers and thus staining valuable documents.

* Have some change to pay for any photocopies you want to make.

* You may be able to take photos of certain documents using a phone or a camera (always turn the flash off and use in silent mode). Check the rules before using.

* Most records will be stored by their parish, manor, hundred or poor law union, and these may not be familiar to you and also might have changed boundaries in the past. Victoria County Histories and records in the library should enable you to confirm them.

county for a fee through the inter-library loan service.) As you start to work your way through some of the more recent and easy to interpret records such as trade directories, make a note of the names of neighbours' houses and any notable buildings close by because, when you reach documents that are earlier than the mid-19th century, your house will not be numbered and may just be referred to as 'Jim Bloggs' house' or 'the house next to the church'. Always cross reference any important facts: many Victorian books refer to events which may have been based upon rumour or tradition since they did not have easy access to the wealth of documents as we do today.

FIRST STEPS

Title deeds

A primary source which you should try to find are the title deeds to the property. These documents confirm previous transfers of the property from one party to another in order to establish ownership. They can include mortgages, court papers and wills. If there is a mortgage on the property, then the deeds will be held by the lender (i.e. building society or bank), and it is usually possible to get copies from them. If the house is owned outright, then the deeds will either have been passed to the owner or left for safekeeping with the solicitor. There is a problem with title deeds, however, because from 1925, to prove ownership one only had to keep records going back 30 years and then from 1970 only 15 years, so this potential rich source may only contain a few recent documents.

If you get lucky and they have survived, then they will not only give you a list of previous owners but also may have details of the very first purchase or when the house was built (do not assume that the first dated document is when the house was constructed; earlier documents may have simply been lost). If your title deeds do not go back further than a few decades, then do not despair, there are other places where they could be found. Ask neighbours or people in the street or estate who own property which appears of a similar age if they have their own deeds as these may contain information about when they were first built. You can check with the solicitors to see if they still have the surplus parts of the deeds in their own records or the lawyers who acted for a previous sale. It is also possible that the deeds were deposited with either the County Record Office or the Public Record Office, now the National Archive (see Chapter 7 for details on accessing these). If you have no access to any documents, then the Land Registry can issue copies of details on the current ownership of a property and these may contain reference to a previous owner.

Family Records

It is also worth checking that there are not any records hidden away in a box in the loft or with distant relatives. If the house has been in your family for some time or you know the previous owner, then there may be old documents, plans or photographs which might be useful in showing how the building has developed or

LEGAL TERMS

The following is a simplified explanation of some of the more common phrases or types of document you can come across on old land documents:

Freehold: Land which was granted to an individual.

Copyhold: Property held with unrestricted service due to the lord of the manor.

Leasehold: A later development where either free or copyhold land could be leased out for a set length of time.

Fee Simple: Land held by a grant to an owner and his heirs which would return to the person who first granted it when this line ran out. It could, however, be taken away or given to someone else in the meantime. Conditions could be applied to this method.

Fee Tail: As for fee simple but the property could not be granted or taken away while there was a family line.

Life Interest: Property held for the life of the person it was granted to, although he could give it away to another but they could only hold it for the same length of time as the original tenant before it reverted to the grantee.

Fee farm: Land granted for a fixed time.

Feoffment: The transfer of a piece of land which was held as fee simple from one person to another.

Deeds of lease: A document which can record amongst other things the transfer of building rights so that the original owner could still get ground rent but the new leaseholder could erect houses and charge rent for them.

Final concord or fine: A fake legal dispute was created between the two interested parties which had to go to court to be resolved, with the final agreement being the concord or fine.

Common recovery: Another method involving a fake legal dispute at the courts, in which the two parties would agree beforehand on a price and exchange money, then the current owner would not turn up at the hearing and the land would default to the new owner.

Bargain and Sale: Method of transfer which maintained the lord of the manor's right to enact service from a tenant when he was the beneficiary of a trust.

Lease and Release: Similar to above and used from the 17th century to bypass the need to go to court and to avoid owing service to the lord of the manor.

Strict Settlement: A common method of transfer by the 19th century which combined various methods in order to keep the property within the family.

changed. A picture of the façade or of the inside of a room might show original fittings such as windows and fireplaces which have since been replaced and could help with dating; or receipts for building work could highlight new from old parts of the structure. Neighbours might have photographs which include your property and the family solicitor could also have old documents relating to the house.

FIG 6.1: *Boundaries can be important and it can be useful to identify ones which are likely to be old on a map. Look for a low bank and trees with a thick stubby base and numerous shoots as this can be a sign that the hedge was traditionally formed by cutting trees and laying them flat (top). Also count the number of species of flora and fauna in it; each one you find can represent 30 years, so one with ten could be 300-years-old (there are many problems with this method so it is only a very rough guide). Also use the same principles for dating the structure of a building to establish if any walls in the area are very old; many suburban estates were built on the site of an old country house and parts of walls often from the gardens can sometimes be found (bottom).*

Your Surroundings

In addition to recording the property in detail as outlined in the preface, it is also important to walk around the neighbourhood and make yourself familiar with your surroundings. Names of notable buildings, structures which look similar to yours and even lumps and bumps in neighbouring fields can be clues which might be worth investigating or will show up in later research. This has been made all the easier now thanks to Google maps which when using the satellite option gives you a detailed aerial photograph of your community. Although a lot of details may not show up clearly depending on what time of day the photos were taken (these are not live images but can be a number of years old), they are a useful resource for making yourself familiar with the area and identifying features or buildings around yours which may not be visible on the ground.

FIG 6.2: *Although advertised as being built in around 1900 this row of houses appeared earlier and the proof is in the name. Inkerman was a battle in the Crimean War fought in November 1854. After initial enthusiasm for its use in street names it quickly dropped from popularity so the development can be pinpointed to a narrow space in time. Other battles used for street names include Quebec 1759, Camperdown 1797, Trafalgar 1805, Waterloo 1815, Alma 1854, and Sebastopol 1855.*

Names

Another important source of information is the name of the house, terrace or street. Sometimes these can give a surprisingly accurate clue to the date of the property. The name might record a previous

FIG 6.3: *Names of streets and houses can sometimes be changed. When built, this early example of council housing was celebrated by being called Sanitation Street. However, later residents were not so enthusiastic with such a clinical name and had the 'S 'dropped off the front and the 'tion' at the end, so today it is simply Anita Street.*

landowner, use of the land or old building which can help narrow down later research. Some common names include Jubilee or Coronation which can be dated to the time around a royal celebration; victorious battles are often recorded like Waterloo or Sebastapol and sometimes other national or local historic events which can be pinpointed to a certain year. Descriptions of rows or roads change with fashions: for instance 'squares' were common in the late 18th and early 19th centuries, 'street' was very popular in the Victorian period, and 'crescents' in the inter-war years, while 'lane' and 'road' could be an older route now within the urban sprawl (see Fig 1.11). Villas were applied to the finest detached properties in the Regency period but slowly became used more freely and by the late 19th century could be found on modest rows of terraced housing. Sometimes the name implied antiquity like 'grange', which was popular with Victorians but did not always mean that the property had formerly been attached to an abbey (a grange was a monastic farm).

Most fields will also have names which can be very important for those which border a rural property. These may be known to locals and can appear in some of the records which are listed further in the book. They can refer to previous use of the land, perhaps an old building and sometimes a lost village. Interpreting the name can sometimes be tricky but there are catalogues produced by the English Place Names Society which can help (usually there are copies in local studies centres). It is also important to note that names can change over time, and with some old ones the spelling varied each time it was recorded, while others were changed intentionally.

LOCAL STUDIES CENTRE

Ordnance Survey Maps

Maps are some of the most important documents when tracing the history of your house. They have been produced for a number of individuals and bodies since the 15th century but only began to be produced as a complete series covering the country in the early 1800s. This was undertaken by the Ordnance Survey, the

FIG 6.4: *Large-scale Ordnance Survey maps range in scale from 1:500 (left) to 1:10,000 (right) depending on whether they were covering busy urban areas or rural communities. It is helpful if you take along a copy of a modern plan or satellite image of the area around your house when visiting your local studies centre so you can compare it with old maps. Also make a note of the map reference where your house is (i.e. SK 455 347) as this may be useful for later research.*

military's mapping department, producing large-scale maps (the folded sheets you buy in shops are referred to as small scale and are either 1:25,000 or 1:50,000, large-scale maps will be from 1:10,000 up to 1:500) which are big enough to make out individual houses and, unlike many earlier types, were accurate and to scale. These Ordnance Survey maps were revised at regular intervals (with the date of issue on the bottom strip); towns and cities being revised more often than the rural areas. Copies of these should be found in your local studies centre, together with other local maps which may be of interest. Ordnance Survey maps from 1801 are also kept in the National Archives which may be older than those available locally and they also have a large range of other plans and maps (some of which are mentioned in the following chapter).

For anyone with a Victorian or later property, a map can show what the area was like before the house was built and its appearance on a map can indicate that it was constructed some time between this and the previous issue of the map. Also, look at the boundaries: you might find that one section was part of an old hedgerow predating the estate or an odd-shaped garden was formed because of a feature that appears on an early map but has now long since gone. If you are lucky and find a very large scale urban map of your house, then you might even be able to make out details like extensions, outbuildings and garden features. It is important, however, to read the notes along the bottom of each sheet as many revisions were made simply to update railways and roads, with the buildings remaining the same as the previous issue. There may be extra information on the county council's website about accessing and interpreting these maps.

Victoria County History

Another important and easy to access publication is the *Victoria County History* series: they are large red or cream hardback books divided into volumes covering

FIG 6.5: *The Victoria County History is an essential first step and if you are lucky to have your town or village covered there will be a comprehensive history, perhaps even dates when your road was laid out and links to documents where there may be further information. You can also find the hundred, parish and manor which your house is likely to be in which will be important for later research. Details like the manor in which your house falls can be useful. If, for instance, it was monastic lands, then records might be found from before the 1530s stored in the National Archives, or it can tell you if the estate your house was once on was held by someone who resided in another county and hence the records might be there.*

the history of different parts of each county. This is a privately-funded project established in 1899 and dedicated to Queen Victoria, with the intention of publishing a detailed history of a community. Not being a government-backed scheme, however, has meant that this Herculean task and valuable resource has had a troubled existence, and it was only when, in 1933, it was re-housed in the Institute of Historical Research at the University of London that the project became more established.

The coverage is still patchy: some counties have most areas covered, others only a volume or two on aspects of its history, while the West Riding of Yorkshire and Northumberland have yet to be started. Each year a few new red books are produced and as funding is established incomplete areas can be restarted. To find out if your area is covered, visit www.victoriacountyhistory.ac.uk, or try your local studies centre which will have any existing copies. The counties are usually divided into hundreds (Saxon divisions of old shires) which can make it tricky, but there is usually a contents or index available to help. Inside each red book are entries for a parish, including the history of the manors, the church and other important bodies, and in some there are more details on urban development and individual buildings. You might for instance find the dates when roads were laid out or housing estates begun which can be essential for research of more recent houses. There are also lists of documents where the information was found so you can discover even more.

Trade Directories
See Chapter 8

Statutory List of Buildings of Special Architectural or Historic Interest
Any building of note or of a certain age can be listed to protect it for future generations. The listing comes in three levels, Grade II, Grade II* and, for the most

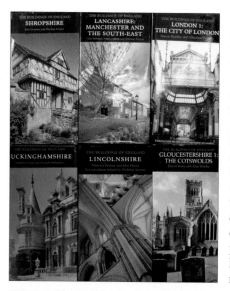

FIG 6.6: The Buildings of England *series initially by Nikolaus Pevsner divided into each county or principal city is a useful aid. Even though the specific house you are interested in may not be mentioned, the background information on local buildings can be very useful.*

important, Grade I. You should be made aware when you purchase a property whether it has been listed. Also, at the time of the listing, a survey would have been made by a local architectural expert and a copy of this can be found within the Statutory List of Buildings of Special Architectural or Historic Interest and kept in either the local studies centre or council planning office. You should also find most listed buildings and structures at www.britishlistedbuildings.co.uk where the details and estimated dates of construction are included for most entries. Remember, however, that the person carrying out the survey may not have had access to documents, could only make opinions on what could be seen, and may not have had access to every part of the building. While some buildings have comprehensive details, others have little more than a few lines stating its main point of interest.

Local history groups usually print annual publications of recent discoveries and studies. You can always join one of these groups, and receive these often fascinating records, or find copies of them in the local studies centre. Although some entries may concern properties older than your house, they may be of interest if they are close by or if they contain studies about a particular aspect of buildings in the area.

The Buildings of England Series

The best series of books to discover more about the houses in your area is the *Buildings of England* by Nikolaus Pevsner, an art historian who from 1945 through to the early 1970s toured towns and villages throughout the country casting his expert eye upon their most notable structures. The books are still being worked on by other experts in the field and reprinted regularly, with some having extra text added to make surprisingly comprehensive studies of buildings which may even include your house or estate. The introduction to each county, which describes the development of its buildings and types of materials, is particularly useful, as well as the entry for your town or village even if your property is not included. Most local studies centres will have a copy of your county's issue and you can find out more information at www.pevsner.co.uk.

Photo Collections and Old Prints

All libraries have numerous books full of old photos of towns and villages dating back to the mid-19th century and, although you would be fortunate to find your house illustrated, unless it was in a prominent central position, they can still be useful in showing how the area developed. The original appearance of similar houses and the notes often written by a local historian can contain facts which might relate to an estate or terrace. Local studies centres and bookshops have old prints of the area, sometimes 17th- and 18th-century maps or old views over the town or village. Although rarely accurate, they can be worth checking to see if your house existed or how the area appeared. Its omission should not be taken as definite proof it was not there, however, since artistic licence was widely used.

Newspapers and Notices

Other gems of information are the copies of old local newspapers held within the local studies centre. Sections listing houses for sale, auction or rent, adverts inviting builders and carpenters to build houses on vacant plots, and news about developments in the area can help establish when a house was built and names of

FIG 6.7: *It is always worth taking a look inside walls, at foundations, studying roof timbers and keeping samples of bricks and materials any time that there is building work going on in the house (take photos too before it is sealed up). The builders may also know of other properties with similar materials or type of construction which could help in dating the house.*

people who may have lived there. They are usually held on microfiche (a single large piece of photographic film) or microfilm (a long strip wound upon a spindle) and can be viewed through reading machines which magnify the image. These are easy to use and staff will always show you how to get started.

Adverts and notices for sales and auctions may also be held in the records of local estate agents or solicitors. If you can find out from maps what was on the land before your house was built, then the notice of the sale of the farm, country house or just vacant land could give a clue as to when the site was developed. If you are very fortunate and find a notice relating directly to your property, then the description of the building and listing of the goods and land included in the sale can help build up a picture of how it may have appeared at the time.

Old Guide Books and Contemporary Literature

Since the early 18th century, books have been published about travels or tours through the countryside which include comments about towns and villages passed en route, and they can be of interest when trying to find out about the local area. In the late 19th and early 20th centuries a large number of guides and local history books were also produced and, because they themselves are now of historic value, they are worth checking, especially if they mention 'houses newly erected' since the year of first publication can help date your property. There are also a number of books covering aspects of local towns and the countryside often divided up into counties which again are worth a look.

If you know roughly when your house was built, then it is worth finding out if there is any contemporary literature, especially if it was written in the local area. The works of Thomas Hardy set in rural Dorset; Dickens in industrial London; and Flora Thompson in north Oxfordshire all have useful details on houses and, although they are fiction, they can help you understand how properties may have appeared at the time and how the people in them lived.

> The above sources are some of the most common which can be of use. However, each library will have surprises: a local history book of great detail, a photocopy of handwritten research into a local building or estate, and books of stories and legends which could refer to particular properties. It is well worth trawling through the shelves to see what else you can uncover. Local studies centres will also have index cards to help you find information and may also have a list of further documents or records which are held in the county and National Archives. It is these sources which we will look at in the next chapter.

CHAPTER 7
The Advanced Search: County and National Archives

If local sources have not answered your questions about how old the property is and who lived there, or you are just interested in learning more about the house, then the next step is to look further afield at records held in county record offices and the National Archives. These will include a wide range of documents, of which the most common and useful for tracing the history of your house are listed in this chapter (those relating to the people who have lived in the house are in chapter 8). Although these collections can seem vast and the nature of many of the records bewildering (not helped by those produced before 1733 being mainly in Latin and dates being vague before the Gregorian calendar was adopted in 1752), access to them and help in understanding the content is widely available, both in the respective offices and on the excellent websites. There are also a number of books which go into more detail about old documents and how to interpret them and these are listed in the bibliography.

County record offices, or archives as they are often known today, are usually sited in the county town; information about them should be on the county council's website. They will contain a wide range of documents which might include the records of local poor laws, the civil parish, town councils, justices of the peace, and transport authorities or companies. The archives of local architects, solicitors, estate agents, major companies and some landed estates may also be found there. Before visiting, note that it may be necessary to book in a space during busy times and you will need to take along proof of identity showing your address in order to pick up a reader's ticket when you get there (the websites will usually tell you the types of details they will require).

The National Archives at Kew, formerly the Public Record Office, will be the most useful source of documents when tracing the history of your house. Principally, it contains the records of government, which will include returns for taxation, maps, surveys of land ownership and records of commissions, all of which are a rich resource in establishing when your property was standing and details about its value. The records held there will have a reference which will start with the initials of the department (eg: IR = Inland Revenue). It also has an excellent website, www.nationalarchives.gov.uk, and many of the most common documents can be viewed and copies ordered online so a visit in person may not be required.

OTHER ARCHIVES

There are a number of other archives and collections which hold records of interest when tracing the history of your house:

British Library

Visit their online catalogue to find out if they have anything of interest. Although you are welcome to visit the library, the reading rooms have limited access and reading tickets will probably only be issued to the public if they can prove that the information is not held in any other collection (the staff there can help you in finding this out). Visit their website for more information, www.bl.uk. The main library is at 96 Euston Road, London NW1 2DB and they have another site at Boston Spa, Wetherby, West Yorkshire LS23 7BQ. The British Library Newspaper Collection is also part of the library and is held at Colindale Avenue, London NW9 5HE.

The National Monuments Record Office

This is the public archive of English Heritage and contains records collected by the Royal Commission for Historic Monuments and archaeological surveys and details of some specific buildings. They are located at The Engine House, Fire Fly Avenue, Swindon SN2 2EH and there are more details on www.english-heritage.org.uk/professional/archives-and-collections/nmr. You can put in a request to see if they have any records relating to your house or area though they can take a number of weeks to get back to you.

British Architecture Library

Contains various sources of information like plans, photographs and records of architectural firms and although part of the RIBA it is now open to the public. There is an online catalogue on www.architecture.com/LibraryDrawingsAndPhotographs/RIBALibrary so you can discover if they have anything relating to your property, the architect or firm which built it. The books and periodicals are stored at the RIBA headquarters at 21 Portman Square, London W1 while their drawings and archives are on Level 4 of the Henry Cole Wing at the Victoria and Albert Museum, London.

If you do decide to go there, the records are held at their offices in Kew, south-west London, near to Kew Gardens station (TW9 4DU). You can obtain access to the copies of documents held there without a ticket; you only need one for viewing original records and these can be picked up when you visit (again, check the visiting section of the website for details). The National Archives will allow the use of laptops, mobile phones and cameras and you can take photos of documents that are not susceptible to damage. In order to help find further records when you get to the record offices, it will be useful to take along details not only of document references but also any other names by which the house, neighbours' houses and the road on which they are sited, were known.

When searching through records online, remember that the title of a document will be listed and not the individual entries so if you cannot find what you are looking for under the house name or owner, then try putting in the type of record and your town or village to see if that helps. Also do not lose heart if your property is not listed on a certain document despite being sure it stood at that time; its absence may be of interest as it might mean it was below a certain threshold (perhaps it did not have enough windows to be included in the Window Tax) and therefore might tell you something about the size or value of the house. It is also possible that mistakes have been made in transcribing the information into a digital format, so try a different spelling of a name to see if that makes a difference.

THE RECORDS

Valuation Office Survey or Lloyd Georges Domesday

This was a survey carried out as part of the 1909–1910 Finance Act in order to establish the real value of land; this was so that government could tax landowners for any increase in its value due to public works such as new roads. The country was divided up into valuation districts within which surveyors carried out visits to all properties and recorded details, including the names of owners, the type of property, its tenure and other buildings on the site. They produced working plans and revenue books (known as Domesday Books), and those which have survived should be in your county record office. A final copy of the plan and a field book was made once the survey was complete and is now stored at the National Archives. Visit www.nationalarchives.gov.uk for more details about the Act, surveys and access to the records.

Maps

Maps have been produced for a wide variety of reasons over the centuries and in addition to the Ordnance Survey maps held in your local studies centre, there are

FIG 7.1: *Tithe maps are generally accurate and similar in appearance. Many have the houses coloured in red and outbuildings in grey. The numbers in each lot relate to the accompanying tithe apportionment which lists the size of the plot and information on the owner.*

FIG 7. 2: *Two maps showing how parliamentary enclosure affected a village, with the old field system replaced by groups of fields around new isolated farms and the loss of common land and sometimes housing. The enclosure maps which were produced as part of the process only tend to appear from the late 18th century and they can vary in appearance so there is no standard plan. Records of enclosure acts were stored with the clerk of the peace and are generally held in county record offices.*

others of interest in county and national archives. When the payment of tithes (traditionally a proportion of your produce or income given to support the local church and priest) was changed to an annual payment after the Tithe Commutation Act of 1836, a map was produced to show the divisions of parish land in numbered portions. These relate to the accompanying Tithe Apportionment which included details about the owners. A copy of the tithe maps may be found in county record offices and another should also be in the National Archives although not all areas were covered or have survived. Records of tithe liability may also be found in these archives or online which contain details of owners.

Parliamentary enclosure acts transformed villages and the surrounding landscape over much of England during the Georgian and Victorian periods, and the records produced and the maps which tend to accompany them detail much of the change which took place. Most of the areas affected were across central England and not all the records survive and then only usually from the late 18th century. Those which have survived should be in the county record office although there are some in the National Archives. They may not contain much information beyond showing if the house existed and its boundaries but they are a fascinating look into the development of rural communities.

Maps were sometimes produced for an estate and these also are usually found in the county record office although do note that they might be in the county of the main estate and not necessarily where your property is located. Maps were also produced when a railway, main road, reservoir or other major scheme was planned. If your property is close to one of these, then it is worth checking online catalogues and at your county record office to see if any survive. Those for railways should be in the National Archives. You may need to find out which company built the line; the Victoria County History may help and there are always local railway history books in the local studies centre. Others for major changes which affected the community should be in the county record office. Houses which are inside or near to military sites may also be included on planning maps. The Imperial War Museum may be a good first contact (Lambeth Road, London SE1 6HZ).

National Farm Survey

At the outbreak of the Second World War the Ministry of Agriculture and Fisheries sought to increase crop and dairy production. In order to find out where improvements could be made they commissioned a survey of all farms (over five acres) from June 1940 until early the following year. This was followed by further surveys which would form the background to post war planning. The records taken and the maps produced are very useful if your house is in the countryside as they will show both a plan of the property and also who owned it, for how long and the nature of the tenure. They are stored at the National Archives; the records are in the series MAF 32, and the maps are in MAF 73 (there are further details on their website and you can search the catalogue to get the reference for your parish).

Taxation

The records of various forms of taxation can form a useful source of information when tracing the history of a house. Most will contain information on the owner or tenant and often will include details of the house itself, since the tax assessment was often based on the nature of the property. Some of the important ones are listed here.

FIG 7. 3: *The Hearth tax is useful because it lists the number of fireplaces and chimneys which the house had at the time and, assuming you are confident your house was standing when it was compiled, it will be an insight into its form. Entries are listed by owner or tenant in an area so you will usually need further research to establish which one is yours and as in this example they are simply listed as chargeable or not chargeable with the number of hearths they had.*

The Hearth tax (also known as Chimney tax or money) was introduced in 1662 to raise funds to support the recently restored royal household. It was seen at first as a fair way of assessing the amount of tax to charge as the larger houses of the wealthy would have more hearths and chimneys. However, many important landowners had sufficient influence to avoid it and the middle classes, which it hit the hardest, resented it such that it was repealed by William and Mary when they took the throne in 1689 (in part to raise their own popularity). The records of the receivers – or chimney men as they were known – will vary but their assessments usually include the name of the householder and the number of hearths in the property which can be useful in judging the form of the building at the time and wealth of the owner (beware that it could, of course, relate to an earlier house on the site). There were exemptions at the time for the very poor although properties may still have been recorded; private kilns, furnaces and ovens were not included in the tax. Most records are held within the National Archives under the E179 database which you can check for your parish online. There has been a lot of research into these records and books published by local history societies so you might find the records easier to access in these, copies of which are also stored at the National Archives. (London Hearth Tax returns are now being made available online.)

Land tax was introduced in 1692 with a fixed amount charged to each county. Local assessors would then calculate who would have to pay what to make up the allocated figure. It was the owner who was usually charged (some rental agreements made the tenant pay) and records might include their names and the value of land and amounts charged. Any records which survive are likely to be in the county record office, especially those after 1780 when payment was linked to the right to vote. The details were kept in the quarter session rolls (the records of the county justices who met four times a year, hence 'quarter'). There is one collection for the late 1790s in the National Archives.

Window tax was notorious and very unpopular from when it was introduced in 1696 until its repeal in 1851. It was initially charged on houses with over ten windows, but this was dropped to seven from 1766 and then raised to eight from 1825. The records of this are not so easy to access, or so useful, as other taxes and there were exceptions from payment to further compound the problem. Those which do survive should be in the county record office.

House tax, which was charged on the number of occupants in a house that were liable to pay parish church or poor rates, was collected alongside Window tax (until 1834) and any records from this will again be in the county records office.

Title Deeds

In addition to the title deeds which you can retrieve for your property (see Chapter 6), there may also be a few in the county and national archives. Some methods of conveyancing property involved the courts (see Chapter 6) and registers and copies of deeds were made and can still be found in county record offices. Sometimes the originals were never collected after a hearing and are therefore in the National Archives. If the property was on Crown lands or the Crown came into possession of it, then there may be further records in the National Archives, and houses which formed part of an estate or were owned by the church might have their deeds stored in the county or diocesan records office.

Manorial Records

Documents created by a manor, including court rolls, surveys, maps, accounts and records of tenants can be hard to find. Much of the country was not under the feudal system so there will be little for these areas and where they were created, survival is patchy and their locations are varied. However, the Manorial Documents Register, which is now in the National Archives and can be accessed online, is a simple way of tracking down where they might be deposited. This is still in the process of being computerised so if your county is not yet covered, you will have to approach them directly to see what is available. The Victoria County History will also have notes of which manorial documents were used in compiling it and where they were located.

The actual documents will usually be found in either the county record office (for the county where the manor itself was sited), or may still be in the hands of the estate whether it was a private individual or a body like a university. For ecclesiastical records the Church of England Records Centre, London SE16, or the Church Commissions Record Office, 1 Millbank, London SW1 are good starting points. Manors which were in Crown hands will have their records in the National Archives. The most useful documents are those which record tenure, especially ones which were copyhold and a change of occupier resulted in details like the names of

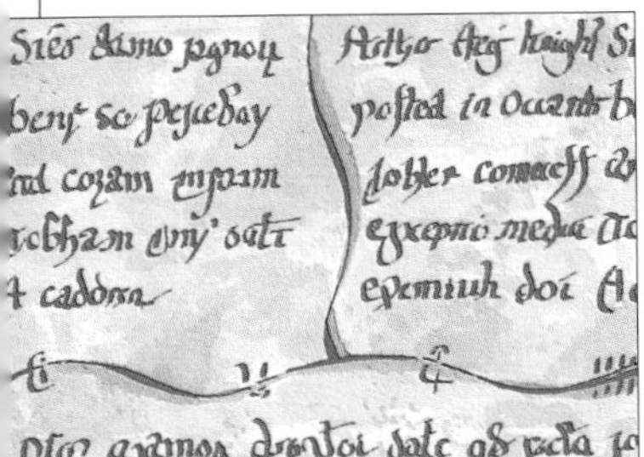

FIG 7.4: *A popular method of conveyancing in the past was to create a fictitious legal dispute between the person wishing to obtain the land (the querent) and the one selling it (the deforciant) which would have to be heard at the Court of Pleas. The final agreement was written out on parchment with the querent's and deforciant's copies side by side (top left and right) and the third part (along the bottom) retained by the courts (hence known as the feet of fines). It was then divided up by cutting it, usually with a wavy line, so only the genuine sections could match up with the official copy. These feet of fines have sometimes found their way into the National Archives and they have a collection from the medieval period up until 1839.*

tenants old and new and the nature of the property being recorded in the manorial court rolls, with a copy given to the tenant (hence 'copyhold'). There may also be records made when copyhold land was converted to freehold mainly during the 19th century and these can be found at the National Archives.

Trade and Industry

As trade with the rest of the world boomed in the 18th century so many who worked in ports and coastal districts became wealthy and may have had a number of properties. The records of men, most notably merchants, will often be found in the local or county record office, if not then the archivists may know where the records of a company or individual have been deposited. For instance, some are in the India Office Records section at the British Library. (Note that ports were heavily bombed in the Second World War and many records were lost.)

In the 19th and 20th centuries large industries and factories often had housing built for their workers and the details of these properties may still be stored within the records of a nationalised or recently privatised company or may have been deposited in a local heritage or county archive. Many of the records for large industries like the railways or coal board are stored in the National Archives,

---

DENDROCHRONOLOGY

All houses use timber in some parts. Although the form and details like joints can give clues to dating they can rarely be precise. However, an ingenious solution has been developed in recent decades which can date an individual piece of timber to not just a year but even the season it was felled! This is based on the fact that ring growth within the tree is greater or smaller depending upon the weather and climate in a particular year and as a tree grows it, in effect, forms a bar code of local climatic change. By studying and recording this pattern from known sources, samples can be compared and matched and a date for felling established. This is, however, a developing science and there are limitations depending on region and at the moment it only works with oak and some conifers. If you have a timber-framed house, then this could be an excellent way of dating the structure. A dendrochronology service is offered by some universities and private companies (try 'dendrochronology services' on your search engine). However, it will be best to start by reading the guidelines on the subject from English Heritage (this is free from the Scientific Dating Section, English Heritage, 23 Savile Row, London W1X 1AB, tel. 020 7973 3000) as there may be issues with listed buildings and establishing the type of timber. A number of core samples will be taken from timbers in the house (holes can be left open or plugged) and then prepared and compared in laboratories to find dates when trees were felled. Costs can be in the region of £500–£1000 but are cheaper if you get it done when building work is going on and timbers are being cut or are more accessible.

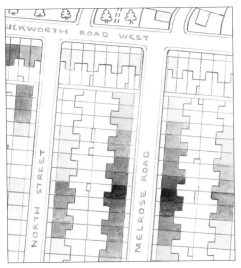

FIG 7.5: *Bomb damage maps as shown here in this replica were produced in London from a bomb census carried out from late 1940 to record which type of bomb had fallen and the destruction caused so this could be used to help in planning later reconstruction. The colours indicated the degree of damage, with houses marked in light yellow suffering little up to those in dark purple which had been flattened. Other cities had similar schemes and the original census records are held in the National Archives.*

URBAN RECORDS

In addition to the more general records already listed, there may be some which are usually associated with urban properties and will usually be stored within county records offices:

- Records of local and county justices might include issues involving tenants of your property, including details of payments made for encroachment of a property that fronts onto a high street or market place.
- Alehouse recognisances or bonds preserved from 1780–1828 record publicans if your property was licensed.
- From 1689 until 1852 houses used by religious dissenters had to be registered with the quarter sessions and records will be in county records offices. Information was transferred to the Registrar General after this date and is in the National Archives (RG31). Roman Catholic places of worship were also registered after 1791 and will be found in the same places.
- Rates were charged in the past to support the parish poor, road maintenance and the church. Records of these sometime survive although usually only with the names of parishioners and not the houses. The county records office may contain documents relating to later 19th-century rates and when they were first charged, and also records of the poor law union and sewer rates.
- Houses affected by road diversions and closures were documented from 1697.
- After the 1715 Jacobite uprising, papists had to register their names and description of home.
- Plans for council houses and subsidised rural housing may also be stored in local or county records offices.

FIG 7.6: *Saltaire was a model community developed in the 1850s and 1860s next to Titus Salt's mill to house workers. Like other later schemes the records of the houses can be found in archives on site and in the local studies centre of the town or city within which they were established. In this case there are records at the Saltaire Archive at Shipley College, some on display in The History of Saltaire exhibition in Salt's Mill, and at the local studies centre in Bradford library.*

although it is best if you know the name of the original company which was responsible for providing the housing before it was taken over or was nationalised. As mentioned in the map section, plans and proposals for new canals, river navigations, harbours and railways often included details on houses close by and these could be included in parliamentary records held within the National Archives.

FIG 7.7: *Aerial photos from 1930s onwards might show a house before post war developments. Try Cambridge University Committee for Aerial Photography, private collections like Hunting Aerofilms of Borehamwood, and the O.S. and R.A.F. photos in the National Monuments Record. The U.S. national archives has records of Luftwaffe aerial photos of southern England. They are also useful for identifying previous land use with details like old boundaries, ridge and furrow, or archaeological sites showing up in low sunlight or as crop marks.*

Modern Records

Although most of the records listed so far date from the early 20th century or before, more recent documents and plans may still be of some use when tracing the history of a house. Since the First World War there have been numerous large-scale clearances and redevelopments of what were regarded as slum areas. If the property in question is a council house or within the area of one, then the records of these should be listed by the local authority in the National Archives. If your house is in a garden city such as Letchworth, Welwyn, or a post-war new town like Crawley, Stevenage, Corby, Peterlee or Milton Keynes (even if the house pre-dates the development), then records and plans which will include

FIG 7.8: *There is a growing interest in and appreciation of post-war prefabs, especially now that so few remain. If you are looking for more information on a house you currently live in or one which has disappeared, then the National Archives is the best starting point as the inspiration and funding came from central government and hence the records of how the prefabs were developed, financed and built can be found here. Also try an Internet search engine as there are many groups collecting photos and memories online of prefabs.*

existing buildings should be in the local heritage county records and the National Archives.

Another useful source which can help you piece together how a house developed are old planning applications. The records to gain permission to build an extension or convert a property usually include details on its former state and can be a vital source not only in helping you identify more recent parts of the structure but also in the clues to its former use, previous owners and the appearance of the building at the time.

FIG 7.9: *Before the days of an efficient public fire brigade, houses could be protected by an insurance company who would have its own fire engines which would come to your house when a fire was reported. To make sure it knew which house was insured, the company supplied a metal plate with its emblem and the number of the insurance schedule which was fixed to the outside of the building. If you have one of these for your house, then it may be possible to trace important details about it in the company records stored either in the local library or records offices (the Sun and Royal Exchange are in the Guildhall Library in London and Royal Phoenix at Cambridge University Library, for instance). However, be warned, many of these plates have been fixed to houses in more recent times as decoration and yours may not be for that property.*

CHAPTER 8
Personal Records:
Who Lived in the House?

The possible sources of information listed in the previous two chapters will include the names of the numerous people who have lived or owned your house in the past. There are, however, a few sources which, although by including an address can confirm that a property existed at a certain date, primarily contain information about the occupier. The growth in family history websites and publications also means that finding out the names of past residents is much easier and a lot of the information is available locally or via the Internet. This chapter lists some of the most useful sources of information when trying to find out more about people who have lived in your house.

Census Returns
After 100 years have elapsed, the returns from the once-a-decade national census can be made available to the public. Therefore, the records for 1911 and all previous censuses dating back to 1801 can now be accessed. The early records are of limited use, but from 1841 they include the property and the people living in it

The following sites and magazines are some of the most popular and have access to numerous records which can help trace individuals rather than a property.

Web sites:
www.ancestry.co.uk
www.findmypast.co.uk
www.genesreunited.co.uk
www.ukbmd.org.uk
www.bbc.co.uk/history/trail/familyhistory
www.genuki.org.uk

Magazines:
Family History Monthly: www.familyhistorymonthly.com
Who Do You Think You Are: www.whodoyouthinkyouaremagazine.com
Family Tree Magazine: www.family-tree.co.uk
Your Family History: www.your-familyhistory.com
Your Family Tree Magazine: www.yourfamilytreemag.co.uk

No of Schedule	ROAD, STREET, &C. and No or NAME of HOUSE	HOUSES				Name and Surname of each Person	RELATION to Head of Family		Age last Birthday		PROFESSION OR OCCUPATION	Employer, Worker, Or Own account	If Working At Home	WHERE BORN	
									Male	Female					
1	Cruso St	1				Alice Hall	Head	Sing		40	Spin Silk Spooler	Worker		Leek-Staffs	
						Anetta d:	Sister	d:		38	Silk Spooler	d:		Leek-Staffs	
						Lucy Ann d:	Sister	d:		26	Dressmaker	Own Account	Home	Leek-Staffs	
						Eliza d:	Sister	d:		24	Milliner Ullin	—d:—	d:	Leek Staff	
2	—d:—	1				James E. Cotor	Head	Wed	50		General Labourer	Worker		Killemore Oxford	
						Fanny d:	Daut	S		29	Fancy Jen		Home	Leek Stafford	

FIG 8.1: *The original copies of census returns are an important piece of information when tracing the history of a house. Although many properties which stood at this time will be simply listed by their house number, those which were recently built might only have a plot number or not be named so you may have to look at other returns or information to establish which house is which. It is also possible for the street names to be spelt incorrectly when they have been digitised, for example this return for Cruso Street was listed as Cruss Street!*

(not the owner) and were more detailed still from 1851. They will record the address, names and occupations, along with other details of those living there on the day on which the census was taken. It is possible, however, if no one was available to hand the sheets back to the enumerator, that your house may not appear on the returns, although it does not mean it did not exist. These sheets were then copied into an enumerator's book and it is this latter copy which has since been transferred onto microfilm and is available online.

Although census records have been stored in local studies centres, county records offices and the family records offices collection (which has been relocated to the National Archives), most people now access them through the Internet. There is a wide variety of sites offering access to the returns with different price packages so it pays to shop around and see which is most appropriate for you. The 1911 census and the 1901 census are widely available and you can usually download a simple typed copy or the more detailed copy of the original but remember again, mistakes can be made in transferring the information onto the typed copy so if your street does not appear then it is worth trying a few different spellings or a different website.

Street and Trade Directories
Before the telephone directory and Yellow Pages were developed, street and trade directories were produced for most towns and cities listing businesses and private residences. Some date from the 18th century but it is the Victorian ones which are more comprehensive. They are available in your local studies centre and county record office (the Guildhall Library has a good collection for London). Street directories tend to give more details, whereas trade directories can tell you if a business was run from your property. Both will give you the names of people living

there so you can build up a record of residents over the years to complement those from census records. Be aware, though, that the records were not always accurate. Entries may have continued after someone had died or a business gone bust and should be cross referenced where possible with other directories (*Kelly's* was the most popular but there were many other companies as well).

Wills and Probate

Those who had wealth and land of value in the past would leave a will: the process in law of administering an estate after a death (sometimes one or two years later) is known as probate. There were two elements: the realty (depending on the tenure this would include the property) and the testament which bequeathed the personality (personal goods in the eyes of the law), hence the phrase 'my last will and testament'. Before 1925, if someone had failed to make a will or it was invalidated, then the realty would go to their heir and the personality to the next of kin (starting with the spouse). After this date both went to the next of kin.

Wills, of course, are common today, but most people in the 19th century and earlier had little in the way of possessions and therefore there will be no record of these. However, as most of the old houses still standing today were built for the better off members of a community, there is a chance of finding a will. They may not tell you much about the property but they can give extra information about the deceased. If you can find the inventory (some will have been deposited in your county record office) which was made a few days after death, it could be a fascinating insight to the wealth and character of the occupier.

Before 1858, wills would have been proved in a church court and the records can be hard to locate. Some will be stored in the indexes of the Prerogative Court of Canterbury which is now within the National Archives or those for York are held in the Borthwick Institute (www.york.ac.uk/library/borthwick/research-support/probate-courts). There may also be records stored in the local studies centre, county records office or they may still be with the title deeds. After 1858 the process of probate was passed to the state and the records unified into a single Calendar Index. This can be searched by postal request to The Postal Searches and Copies Department, Leeds District Probate Registry, York House, York Place, Leeds LS1 2BA (the actual records will be held in regional registries). More information about wills and probate can be found on www.justice.gov.uk/guidance/courts-and-tribunals/courts/probate/family-history.

Electoral Lists and Poll Books

From 1696 to 1872 (when voting became secret), a record was kept of who voted (not who was eligible) in an election and which candidate they chose. This was recorded in a poll book and can include a name, address and who they voted for (they are usually arranged by where the person lived rather than by surname) and they are often stored in the local studies centre and county record office. There are also good collections in the Institute of Historical Research, Guildhall Library, London, and in the British Library (try the publication: *Pollbooks 1696-1872*, and *A Directory to Holdings in Great Britain*, Family History Partnership, 2008).

Electoral registers were compiled from 1832 as an annual list of who was eligible to vote. It should record the names and addresses, as well as extra information like the nature of their right to vote. As they were compiled regularly, they can be very useful in tracing the movement of occupants of your house. However, remember that as with the poll books, until the 1880s, only a minority of the population could vote and women were not allowed to vote until 1918. The registers are usually located in the local studies centre or county record office, although there are some collections available on CD and online (try the publication: *Electoral Registers 1832-1948*, Jeremy Gibson, Family History Partnership, 2008).

Births, Deaths and Marriages

The easiest way to find out more about the people who have lived in your house is to access the records of births, deaths and marriages. Although details have been recorded since 1538 in local parish registers, the information linking them to a specific property may not have been recorded until the 19th century. Therefore, they may only be useful to help discover more about a known occupier or to cross reference details found in other sources. Most are kept in county record offices but access to them is very easy on the Internet now. Try using the sites and magazines listed at the beginning of this chapter.

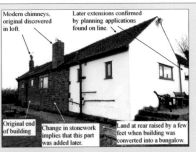

FIG 8.2: *This apparently modern bungalow is a good example which brings together all the aspects of tracing the history of a house. Talking to neighbours, it was established that this was once a two-storey house which had the lower part filled in. An internal inspection verified this with a ledge inside which the floorboards once sat on and ceiling timbers with marks which showed that they had been reused from elsewhere. The loft was revealing as not only did it establish the original form and position of the chimney but also still had lime-washed walls and a bricked-up upper doorway meaning it was probably the granary of a small farm building. Although there was little decorative detail to establish when it was built, an inspection of similar properties of known date in the area imply that it was probably late 18th-century. Documentary evidence was sparse due to the remote location but also because there were three other farms in the parish with the same name! A list of previous occupiers is starting to be formed and new information has just been received at the time of publishing which creates another lead, but as you will find with many houses this is an ongoing project yet to be completed.*

Labels on image: Modern chimneys, original discovered in loft. / Later extensions confirmed by planning applications found on line. / Original end of building / Change in stonework implies that this part was added later. / Land at rear raised by a few feet when building was converted into a bungalow.

SECTION III

FURTHER
INFORMATION

QUICK REFERENCE GUIDE

The following websites can be useful when researching the history of a house. If you do not want to get involved with documentary research, then there are professional researchers who will do this for you. Those listed here are just suggestions and have not been investigated: the publisher and the author take no responsibility for the quality or value of their service.

Documentary research
www.nationalarchives.gov.uk
www.bl.uk (British Library)
www.debrettancestry.co.uk
www.iwm.org.uk (Imperial War Museum)
www.hiddenhousehistory.co.uk
www.british-history.ac.uk (Victoria County History online)
www.victoriacountyhistory.ac.uk
www.englishheritage.org.uk/professional/archives-and collections/nmr (National Monuments Record)
www.justice.gov.uk/guidance/courts-and-tribunals/courts/probate/family-history

Family History
www.ancestory.co.uk
www.genesreunited.co.uk
www.findmypast.co.uk
www.ukbmd.org.uk
www.bbc.co.uk/history/trail/family

History
www.genuki.org.uk

Architecture
www.bricksandbrass.co.uk
www.britishlistedbuildings.co.uk
www.pevsner.co.uk
www.buildinghistory.org
www.architecture.com/LibraryDrawingsAndPhotographs/RIBALibrary

Professional Researchers
www.house-detectives.co.uk
www.house-history-research.co.uk
www.sra-uk.com
www.housestories.co.uk
www.achievements.co.uk
www.pastsearch.co.uk
www.ancestors.co.uk
www.wilsoncomptonassociates.co.uk
www.myhousehistory.co.uk
www.scotsfamily.com

Maps
www.old-maps.co.uk
www.historymaps.co.uk
www.cassinimaps.co.uk

Timecharts: The following pages show periods, styles, leading architects and illustrations of characteristic features of houses in a chronological order.

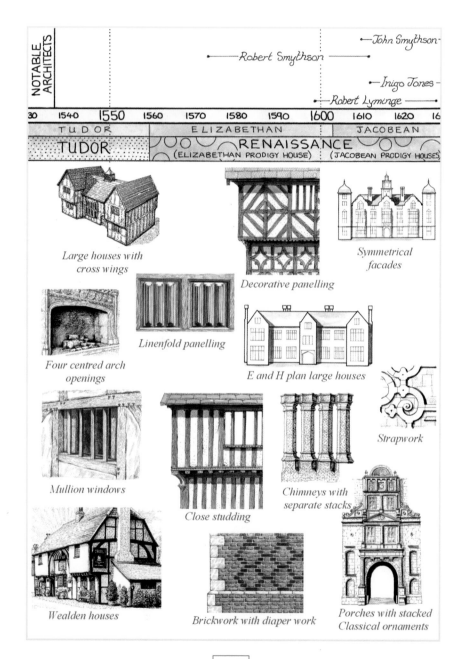

NOTABLE ARCHITECTS

— John Smythson —

— Robert Smythson —

— Inigo Jones —

— Robert Lyminge —

30 1540 1550 1560 1570 1580 1590 1600 1610 1620 16

TUDOR   ELIZABETHAN   JACOBEAN

TUDOR   RENAISSANCE
(ELIZABETHAN PRODIGY HOUSE) (JACOBEAN PRODIGY HOUSES)

Large houses with cross wings

Decorative panelling

Symmetrical facades

Four centred arch openings

Linenfold panelling

E and H plan large houses

Strapwork

Mullion windows

Close studding

Chimneys with separate stacks

Wealden houses

Brickwork with diaper work

Porches with stacked Classical ornaments

John Webb

Hugh May

Sir Roger Pratt

William Talman

Sir John Vanbrugh

Nicholas Hawksmoor

Lord Burlington

Colen Campbell

James Gibbs

| 30 | 1640 | 1650 | 1660 | 1670 | 1680 | 1690 | 1700 | 1710 | 1720 | 17 |

| JACOBEAN | COMMONWEALTH | RESTORATION | WILLIAM + MARY / ANNE | GEORGIAN |

RENAISSANCE (CAROLEAN) (DUTCH STYLE) BAROQUE

English bonding

Large windows and hood moulds

Cross windows

Early sash windows

Brickwork in South and East

Terraces with dormers, sash windows and string mouldings

Classical panelling

Narrow overlights and panelled doors introduced

Bolection moulding

Hoods above doors

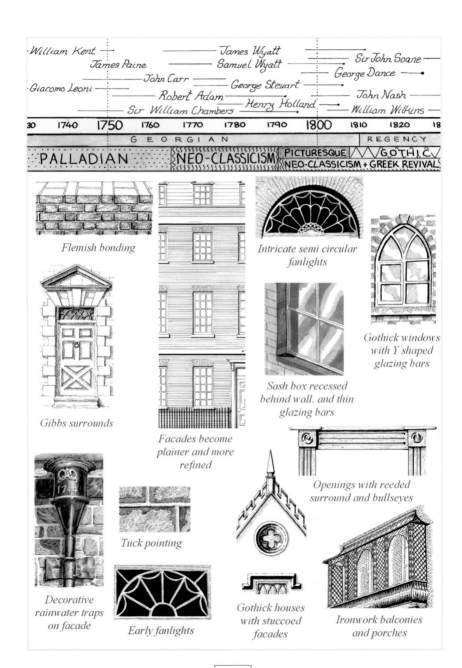

William Kent
James Paine
Giacomo Leoni
John Carr
Robert Adam
Sir William Chambers
James Wyatt
Samuel Wyatt
George Steuart
Henry Holland
Sir John Soane
George Dance
John Nash
William Wilkins

| 30 | 1740 | 1750 | 1760 | 1770 | 1780 | 1790 | 1800 | 1810 | 1820 | 18 |

GEORGIAN · REGENCY

PALLADIAN · NEO-CLASSICISM · PICTURESQUE · GOTHIC · NEO-CLASSICISM + GREEK REVIVAL

Flemish bonding

Intricate semi circular fanlights

Gothick windows with Y shaped glazing bars

Gibbs surrounds

Sash box recessed behind wall. and thin glazing bars

Facades become plainer and more refined

Openings with reeded surround and bullseyes

Decorative rainwater traps on facade

Tuck pointing

Early fanlights

Gothick houses with stuccoed facades

Ironwork balconies and porches

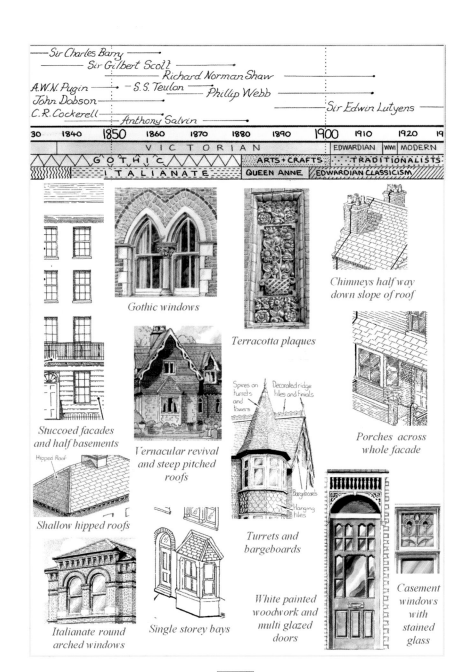

Sir Charles Barry

Sir Gilbert Scott

Richard Norman Shaw

A.W.N. Pugin — S.S. Teulon

Phillip Webb

John Dobson

C.R. Cockerell

Anthony Salvin

Sir Edwin Lutyens

| 30 | 1840 | 1850 | 1860 | 1870 | 1880 | 1890 | 1900 | 1910 | 1920 | 19 |

VICTORIAN · EDWARDIAN · WWI · MODERN

GOTHIC · ARTS + CRAFTS · TRADITIONALISTS

ITALIANATE · QUEEN ANNE · EDWARDIAN CLASSICISM

Gothic windows

Terracotta plaques

Chimneys half way down slope of roof

Stuccoed facades and half basements

Hipped Roof

Vernacular revival and steep pitched roofs

Spires on turrets and towers · Decorated ridge tiles and finials

Bargeboards

Hanging tiles

Porches across whole facade

Shallow hipped roofs

Turrets and bargeboards

Italianate round arched windows

Single storey bays

White painted woodwork and multi glazed doors

Casement windows with stained glass

BIBLIOGRAPHY

B elow is a list of my books covering most periods of housing within this series. They are all fully illustrated with more details about the structure, style and interiors of period houses. More information can be found on my website (www.trevoryorke.co.uk) and they can be purchased through the publisher's website (www.countrysidebooks.co.uk) and through leading book suppliers and shops:

Timber Framed Houses Explained, 2010
Tudor Houses Explained, 2009
Georgian and Regency Houses Explained, 2007
The Victorian House Explained, 2005
The Edwardian House Explained, 2006
1930s Houses Explained, 2006
The 1940s and 1950s House Explained, 2010

Period House Fixtures and Fittings 1300–1900, by Linda Hall, (Countryside Books, 2005) contains a unique collection of illustrations helping to date details especially of 16th- and 17th-century houses.

The *Buildings of England* series by Nikolaus Pevsner and others is divided into counties, with useful information on regional architecture and notable buildings, including houses.

There are a large number of books which go into great detail about documentary research. A few of the more approachable ones are listed here, but make sure that whichever ones you refer to are the latest edition: works on family history and their websites are constantly changing:

Tracing the History of Your House: The Building, the People, the Past, Nick Barratt, 2006
Tracing Your Home's History, Anthony Adolph, (Collins, 2006)
How to Research your House, Every Home Tells a Story: Pamela Brooks, (How To Books Ltd., 2007)
How to Research Local History: Find Out All About Your House, Village or Town, Pamela Brooks, (How To Books Ltd., 2008)
Discovering Local History, David Iredale and John Barrett, (Shire Publications Ltd.,1999)
Starting Out in Local History, Simon Fowler, (Countryside Books, 2001)

There are further publications which specialize in certain aspects of research and can usually be found within the appropriate section of the websites listed at the beginning of this section.

Architrave: The moulding around a door, window or niche.

Ashlar: Smooth, squared stone masonry with fine joints.

Axial: A feature located or a plan laid out along the axis of a house.

Baluster: Plain or decorated post supporting the stair rail.

Balustrade: A row of decorated uprights (balusters) with a rail along the top.

Bargeboard: External vertical boards which protect the ends of the sloping roof on a gable and often decorated (many are Victorian in date).

Baulk: A regional term for a large timber beam.

Bay: A vertical division of a house between trusses; usually reflected on the façade by a column of windows.

Bay window: A window projecting from the façade of a house up a single or number of storeys and usually resting on the ground.

Beam: A large horizontal timber.

Bitumen: A petroleum derivative used for waterproofing flat roofs and forming a damp proof layer in walls or under floors.

Bonding: The way bricks are laid in a wall with the different patterns formed by alternative arrangements of headers (the short ends) and stretchers (the long side).

Bow window: A vertical projection (bay) of a shallow semicircular or a segment of a circle (segmental) in plan.

Bressummer: A term which can refer to a number of horizontal beams but especially the one on the bottom of the upper wall of a jettied building.

Bridging beam: A large beam running down the centre of the ceiling into which the joists are fixed (also known as a summer). It usually has chamfered or moulded lower edges.

Buttress: A vertical support angled up against a wall. Arts and Crafts types tended to have a steep slope down its full height.

Capital: The decorated top of a Classical column.

Cames: Lead work which holds the small panes (quarries) of glass in a window.

Casement window: A window which is hinged along one side.

Cast-iron: A brittle metal formed in moulds, whereas wrought iron is pliable and forged into decorative patterns.

Cill: see sill

Chimneypiece: An internal fireplace surround.

Cornice: A moulding which runs around the top of an external or internal wall.

Coving: A large concave moulding which covers the joint between the top of a wall and ceiling, or under a projecting window.

Crucks: Two slightly bent large timbers set resting upon each other to make an arched support to hold the roof. The individual timbers are known as crucks blades.

Dado: The lower section of a wall. The moulding along the top of this is the dado rail.

Damp proof membrane (DPM): A waterproof barrier incorporated within walls and ground floors to stop rising damp penetrating the structure above (introduced in the late Victorian period).

Dormer window: An upright window set in the angle of the roof and casting light into the attic rooms.

Dutch gables: A gable with concave and convex quadrants and triangles.

Eaves: The section of the roof timbers under the tiles or slates where they project over the wall, often with a fascia board which supports the guttering.

Façade: The main vertical face of the house.

Fenestration: The arrangement of windows in the façade of a house.

Fielded: The raised central part of a panel.

Finial: An ornamental piece on top of a railing or the end of the roof ridge.

Flue: The duct for smoke from the fireplace up into the chimney.

Fluting: The vertical concave grooves running up a column or pilaster.

Frieze: The middle section of the entablature, in this context referring to the section of the wall between the picture rail and cornice.

Gable: The pointed upper section of wall at the end of a pitched roof.

Glazing bars: The wooden or metal divisions of a window which support the panes.

Gothic: Medieval architecture which used the pointed arch.

Gothic Revival: The rediscovery of Gothic architecture which was championed by Pugin and Ruskin and dominated building from the 1850s to 1870s.

Gothick: A less accurate and more whimsical form of Gothic which was popular in the late 18th and early 19th centuries; characterised by wide arched windows with Y-shaped tracery.

Guilloche: A decorative pattern made from two twisted bands forming circles between.

Half timbering: Another popular term for timber-framed construction. In some cases, used to refer to a building with stone or brick lower storey and timber-framed upper.

Hanging tiles: Clay tiles hung vertically off thin strips of wood to cover walls.

Hearth: The stone or brick base of a fireplace.

Herringbone: Brickwork laid in a zigzag pattern.

Hipped roof: A roof with a slope on all four sides.

Inglenook: A recessed space for a fire, with seating to the sides.

Jambs: The sides of an opening for a door or window.

Jetty: The projection of an upper storey of a timber-framed building.

Joggle: Stone blocks with notch on one face and matching recess on the other to prevent them slipping.

Joists: Timber, concrete or steel beams which support the floor.

Lintel: A flat beam which is fitted above a door or window to take the load of the wall above.

Load bearing: A wall which has to support a load, usually referring to a thick internal wall which helps support the roof timbers.

Mansard roof: A roof formed from two slopes at a different angle with a profile like the top of a 50 pence piece which allows more height for a room within.

Moulding: A decorative strip of wood, stone or plaster.

Mullion: The vertical member dividing up a window. A low, long window with only mullions is known as a mullion window.

Muntin: A strip of wood or metal separating and holding panes of glass in a window.

Newel: The principal vertical post in a set of stairs.

Oriel: A large projecting window supported from the wall on an upper storey.

Panelling: Wooden lining of interior walls, with vertical muntins and horizontal rails framing the panels.

Parapet: The top section of wall which continues above the sloping end of the roof.

Pargetting: A raised or incised pattern formed in plaster on an external wall (popular originally in the East of England).

Pebbledash: Render with small pebbles and stones thrown against it while drying.

Pediment: A low pitched triangular feature supported by columns or pilasters above a Classically-styled door or window in this context.

Pilaster: A flat Classical column fixed to a wall or fireplace and projecting slightly from it.

Pitch: The angle by which a roof slopes. A plain sloping roof of two sides is called a pitched roof.

Plinth: The low stone or brick base around a timber-framed building.

Post: A large vertical load bearing timber.

Purlin: A horizontal timber beam which runs along the pitch of a roof.

Quoin: The corner stones at the junction of stone or brick walls.

Rafters: Timbers which are set in a row along the slope of the roof with laths running across their upper surface onto which the tiles are fixed.

Rail: A lesser horizontal timber usually infilling between main posts and beams.

Reeding: Vertical grooves in a door or fireplace surround which were popular in the Regency period.

Render: A protective covering for a wall made from two or three layers of cement.

Reveal: The sides (jambs) of a recessed window or door opening.

Roughcast: A render with small stones mixed within to give a rough texture when dried.

Sash window: A window of two separate sashes which slide vertically (or horizontally on smaller Yorkshire sash windows).

Screed: A mix of sand and cement used to pour over and form the upper layer of the ground floor.

Sill (or cill): The horizontal timber beam at the bottom of the wall which usually rests upon a brick or stone plinth.

Skirting: The protective strip of wood at the base of a wall.

Strapwork: Flat bands which form decorative patterns from the 1580s –1620s.

String: The side support panel for a staircase.

String course: A horizontal band running across a façade and usually projecting.

Stud: A lesser vertical timber usually infilling between main posts and beams.

Terracotta: Fine clay moulded and fired into decorative pieces usually left unglazed on Arts and Crafts buildings.

Tracery: The ribs which divide the top of a window and are formed into patterns.

Transom: A horizontal bar in a window.

Truss: An arrangement of timber or steel pieces incorporating triangles to form a long beam or support for a roof. When carefully designed they can stretch further than a single beam.

Vaulting: A ceiling of stone or brick formed into arches and often found in the basement of large 17th- to 19th-century houses. A few of medieval origin can be found often supported on columns.

Vernacular: Buildings made from local materials in styles and method of construction passed down within a distinct area, as opposed to architect -designed structures made from mass produced materials.

Voussoir: The wedged shaped stones or bricks which make up an arch.

Wainscot: Timber lining of internal walls or panelling.

Wall plate: The main horizontal timber which runs along the top of the wall and under the eaves.

Weatherboarding: Overlapping horizontal planks used to protect timber-framed structures from the elements or disguise poor quality construction.

INDEX